Cooking up
a revolution

MANCHESTER
1824

Manchester University Press

CONTEMPORARY ANARCHIST STUDIES

A series edited by
Laurence Davis, *University College Cork, Ireland*
Uri Gordon, *University of Nottingham, UK*
Nathan Jun, *Midwestern State University, USA*
Alex Prichard, *Exeter University, UK*

Contemporary Anarchist Studies promotes the study of anarchism as a framework for understanding and acting on the most pressing problems of our times. The series publishes cutting-edge, socially engaged scholarship from around the world – bridging theory and practice, academic rigor and the insights of contemporary activism.

The topical scope of the series encompasses anarchist history and theory broadly construed; individual anarchist thinkers; anarchist informed analysis of current issues and institutions; and anarchist or anarchist-inspired movements and practices. Contributions informed by anti-capitalist, feminist, ecological, indigenous and non-Western or global South anarchist perspectives are particularly welcome. So, too, are manuscripts that promise to illuminate the relationships between the personal and the political aspects of transformative social change, local and global problems, and anarchism and other movements and ideologies. Above all, we wish to publish books that will help activist scholars and scholar activists think about how to challenge and build real alternatives to existing structures of oppression and injustice.

Other titles in the series

Cooking up a revolution

Food Not Bombs, Homes Not Jails, and resistance to gentrification

Sean Parson

Manchester University Press

Published by Manchester University Press
Altrincham Street, Manchester M1 7JA
www.manchesteruniversitypress.co.uk

British Library Cataloguing-in-Publication Data
A catalogue record for this book is available from the British Library

ISBN 978 1 5261 0735 0 hardback
ISBN 978 1 5261 4802 5 paperback

First published 2019

The publisher has no responsibility for the persistence or accuracy of URLs for any external or third-party internet websites referred to in this book, and does not guarantee that any content on such websites is, or will remain, accurate or appropriate.

Typeset
by Toppan Best-set Premedia Limited

*I dedicate this book to the activists of Food Not Bombs
and the homeless who have given their time,
energy, and safety to resist gentrification, capitalism,
and state violence.*

CONTENTS

LIST OF FIGURES

ACKNOWLEDGEMENTS

Like any book, there are countless people to thank for their time, insight, and support in making this book a reality. I would like to first thank my parents for their love, kindness, excitement, and copy editing help over the years that I finished my PhD and completed the book. There is also no way I could have completed it without the mentorship and guidance of my dissertation committee—Deborah Baumgold, Gerry Berk, Joe Lowndes, and Michael Dreiling—as well as my friends and colleagues at Northern Arizona University—especially, Geeta Chowdhry, Kim Curtis, Luis Fernandez, John Hultgren, Paul Lenze, Joel Olson, Brian Petersen, Sahar Ravazi, Emily Ray, and Nora Timmerman—for reading and providing comments and insights into the book. Lastly, I would like to thank: Chelsea Green for spending hours listening to me talk about the book, all while providing critical feedback and shaping my thoughts about the world; Brian Lovato and Eli Meyerhoff for your years of friendship and for helping create space within academia for anarchist, abolitionist, and radical political academic and activist work; Michael Lipscomb, Tim Luke, and the members of both the Caucus for New Political Science and the Environmental Political Theory Working Group for providing me space to work and process my ideas; Sway Olvera for providing professional editing and writing support; and Bruno Anili, Clay Cleveland, Ted Duggan, Vanessa Mousavizadeh, Forest Nabors, Abdurrahman Pasha, Josh Plencner, Ed Tayor, and my other friends from graduate school. Finally, I would like to thank the activists from Food Not Bombs and Homes Not Jails—most notably Chris Crass, Diamond Dave, Deborah James, Keith McHenry, James Tracy, and John Viola—who not only gave me their time and their stories but also provided the dedication and passion that has inspired me to fight injustice and struggle for a better world since I was a teenager.

LIST OF ABBREVIATIONS

FNB   Food Not Bombs
GA   General Assistance
HNJ   Homes Not Jail
SF   San Francisco
WTO   World Trade Organization

1

Turning statistics into people: from sick talk to the politics of solidarity

I was intellectually curious but stuck, learning within a boring and hierarchical education system. I had no idea what I believed; all I knew was that I hated the conservative and apathetic political climate I found in San Diego. That culture, the overreliance on cars to traverse the web of highways and the high cost of rental space, meant that there were few radical community centers or infoshops that a carless kid could get to. One of the few exceptions was the Che Café, a radical respite tucked into the woods of the University of California San Diego campus that was also only a short drive or bus ride from my parents' house. The place served as a safe haven for San Diego anarchists, punks, and youth. It is a music venue, vegan coffee shop, anarchist infoshop, and student community space, all rolled into one. In between the bands, and while eating vegan stir-fry, I was introduced to political movements and struggles through spoken-word performances, political documentaries, and activist tabling. It was the place where I first learned about vegan cooking, as you could volunteer to help cook in exchange for paying the cover. Even though the space was small, and I had been going to see shows there since 1996, I had never really explored the Che's zine library. But for some reason in 1998, possibly boredom, I started to peruse the library, and while doing so I saw a flier asking for people to volunteer with San Diego Food Not Bombs. On the flier I saw a picture of a man, who I later learned was Food Not Bombs co-founder Keith McHenry, being led away by riot cops (figure 1.1), with a brief description of the arrests and harassment that the group faced in San Francisco for giving away free food. Emblazoned on the bottom of the flier was the slogan "FOOD IS A RIGHT, NOT A PRIVILEGE." As someone who had volunteered in the café's kitchen multiple times, who grew up in a household where cooking and food—from family dinners to Passover Seders—were central to our identity, and who was in the process of developing a political identity, the flier shocked me into action. It might have been the militant righteousness of Keith McHenry, the fear and anger emanating from the

1.1 Iconic photo of Keith McHenry being arrested by San Francisco police, August 1988

riot cops, or simply the idea that by giving away free food we could change this culture of violence and suffering, but this flier changed my life.

For most of the next fourteen years of my life I was involved, in some way or another, with Food Not Bombs. I remember clearly in early 2001 my friend Mark coming up with the idea that the two of us should start up a chapter in Des Moines. That Sunday we both met up at Mark's dank basement studio and, with the loud screaming of metal blasting through his speakers, we made what two 19-year-olds could make: pasta. After combing our houses for bowls, forks, and cups, we loaded into his Oldsmobile and headed towards Nollen Plaza in downtown Des Moines. For the next three years, every Sunday, I and other friends would meet up at either Mark's house or my house to listen to records and cook. After cooking each week we would drive or bike to downtown and share food with the homeless, poor, and hungry who congregated in the park. In the snow and chilly winds of the Midwest, friendships and relationships blossomed.

It was in the connections and relationships we built during that time that many of us learned the principles of contemporary anarchism. In one instance, we were biking at night around downtown Des Moines when we saw a homeless resident, someone we knew well and had been friends with, being harassed by a police officer near the Des Moines River. He had been forced to sleep outside because he had gone to the shelter drunk and they refused to let him in. Now forced into the streets, this drunken friend was being arrested for public intoxication. We watched and kept an eye on the police officer, as other homeless residents of the city had told us horror stories about police abuse and misconduct. Though we did not stop him from being arrested, the next morning we went to the jail and picked him up, brought him some breakfast and sat together by his makeshift home near the river. On the banks of that river we drank malt liquor and talked. With the cold Des Moines air on my face and the taste of tin on my tongue, we talked about police harassment, his experiences living on the street, and the judgmental intimidation he experienced by businessmen and tourists on a daily basis. This was where I learned the power of solidarity and mutual aid.

Mutual aid, a term coined by the anarchist theorist Peter Kropotkin, has become a central concept to contemporary anarchism. The term simply highlights the fact that humans are not naturally compelled to compete and fight among each other, as Hobbes and other liberals claim. We are not biologically guided to a life that is "nasty, brutish, and short" and do not need the state to keep us in check; we are naturally inclined to help one another. Put simply: as social beings, we have a natural inclination towards social justice. By sharing and taking care of one another, we are engaging in mutual aid—from the flooded streets of New Orleans following Hurricane Katrina, to warm meals on a cold day shared in front of City Hall, to beers on the banks of the Des Moines River. It might seem small, but the act of helping out a friend, listening to their stories when no one else will, and sharing a drink is the perfect exemplification of mutual aid. By caring about each other, we create a community and through that community we support each other during the hard times and celebrate during the good.

Sadly, the forces of global capitalism, white supremacy, and patriarchy have done everything they can to demolish community, to disrupt acts of compassion, and to dismantle any networks of solidarity that exist. This is because genuine grassroots communities can be a threat to the prevailing order, which wants only superficial communities, rooted in the logic of market exchange. The sanitized communities desired by market forces do not threaten the prevailing order and do not offend white middle-class consumers. In the United States, where the political structure has an expressly white supremacist foundation, it is no surprise that the supposed free market tends to be a central node in protecting forces of oppression, and not a tool to undermine them. This is especially the case when property and value are brought into the calculation, since urban space has, throughout US history, promoted the creation of white and middle-class spaces and, as such, capitalism not only promotes a system of market exchanges but also buttresses white supremacy.

In one meal service, shortly after September 11, eggs from a passing SUV pelted me while I held a Food Not Bombs sign. Another time, a man dressed as Uncle Sam with a severed Osama Bin Laden head set up across from the park to counter protest our sharing of vegetable soup. While Uncle Sam's papier-mâché work was fantastic, his message was downright frightening: instead of food and compassion, we need to kill or be killed. It seemed that with the drumbeats of war echoing in the cultural background and the media promoting panic around terrorism, calling for non-violence was too much for some to handle. The nation-state uses fear for its own political end and, as an important philosopher has said, "Fear is the path to the dark side. Fear leads to anger. Anger leads to hate. Hate leads to suffering" (Lucas, 1999). Those in power, those who want to control and exploit, need that fear to maintain our dependence on the security apparatus of the state. Over the years following the invasion of Afghanistan we experienced physical threats, near arrest, and countless accusations of being terrorists ourselves. But we also enjoyed warm soup, vegan pizza, and on a few summer weekends, water balloon fights.

Throughout the years of dumpstering produce, picking up donations, cooking food, and sharing it with the hungry and homeless, I have met hundreds of people, including homeless Vietnam vets, Harvard graduate school dropouts and train-hopping travelers from all over the country. It was through their stories and their friendship that most of my own political world was developed. It was elbow deep into a pile of dirty dishes that I learned the importance of calling oneself a feminist; it was sharing garlic bread with a former black panther member turned Muslim Imam that I learned the history of black nationalism; it was in serving cheese pizza to a vegan train-hopper that I learned about the torture and suffering of female cows in industrial farms; and I learned about democracy, direct and unmediated, through hour long consensus meetings while organizing protests around the World Trade Organization and in opposition to economic globalization. I learned my politics by living them, by fighting for what felt right, and by regularly making mistakes.

My interactions and experiences with the homeless and cast-off members of our capitalist society helped elucidate the way that our system is structured in order to victimize the poor. I heard stories from veterans, injured both mentally and physically, who had gotten stuck in an endless cycle of imprisonment, addiction, and poverty; every time they tried to change their lives an arrest or confiscation of their few meager possessions would force them back into the cycle. I heard horror stories about people being assaulted at the local missions and others being denied a warm place to sleep by the social services of the city because they had been drunk, or accused of being drunk. I met families living in cars after they had been evicted because they did not have rent—often because they had lost their jobs or become overburdened with medical expenses. During these formative years with Food

Not Bombs, I began to reject the political and economic structures that neoliberal capitalism had created.

Food Not Bombs has not just been important to my life, but has touched tens of thousands of other people throughout the world. The group started in Cambridge, Mass in 1980, but there are now nearly 1000 chapters throughout approximately sixty different countries in the world, which means that sometime this week, activists in San Diego, Des Moines, and Jakarta are coming together, experimenting with democracy and collectively sharing vegan food with the poor and hungry, while fighting against the forces of gentrification, militarism, and capitalism. By being a confrontational force against the prevailing order, Food Not Bombs has drawn the ire of police agencies and government authorities (figure 1.2). Activists with the group have been arrested in the majority of major cities in the US and Canada—from New York and San Francisco to Toronto—a large number of small North American towns, and international cities like Moscow and Minsk, for giving away free food to the hungry. The first time I ever went to cook with Food Not Bombs, the activists in the San Diego chapter told me about the group's history, focusing on the group's long history of police harassment, from the struggles between the group and the city of San Francisco to personal stories of activists who had experienced harassment by the local police. Yet in my fourteen or so years organizing with Food Not Bombs in Des Moines, Eugene, Oregon, and San Diego, I rarely experienced police harassment for giving away free food. While we would regularly have police stop by, the only time I was ever even threatened with arrest came in Eugene, when a police officer told me that glass jars were not allowed in the park and that if it breaks and a kid steps on the glass we would be held legally accountable. While such a threat was alarming, it was nothing like the harassment and surveillance faced by the activists that this book is going to detail.

My experience working with Food Not Bombs is not just a story of individual transformation but instead a story of collective resistance to unjust institutions. We collectively strove to create a space of compassion and care, one guided by direct democracy, social empowerment, and non-violence. By embodying the political reality we sought to live in, we engaged in a prefigurative politics that was possibly the most powerful form of propaganda by the deed. By showing that anarchism and direct democracy can exist, even if it was just in a kitchen in a dark basement in Des Moines, we questioned the necessity of the state and did what we could to resist the dehumanizing nature of capitalism. While the actions of Food Not Bombs chapters, from Athens to San Francisco to Kathmandu, might not topple the global capitalist order, they create temporary autonomous zones where we are able to foreshadow the world we want to see.

As my experience in the movement grew, I wanted to understand why it was in San Francisco, of all cities in the country, that a conflict emerged

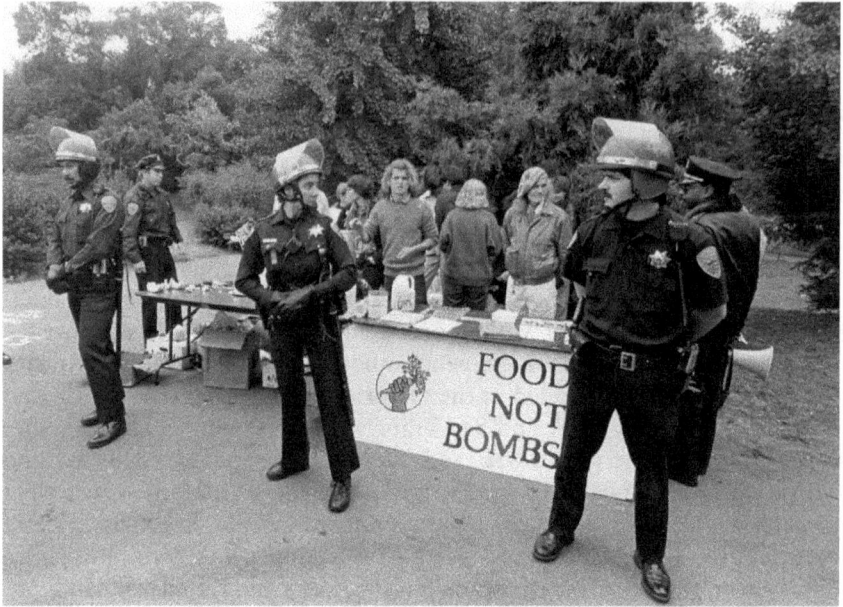

1.2 Riot police blocking a Food Not Bombs table in Golden Gate Park, August 15, 1988

between city officials and Food Not Bombs. What, if anything, did Food Not Bombs do to provoke the antagonistic reaction from the city during this period? Was this conflict productive? Did it help the homeless and poor? Did it do anything to dent the armor of capital?

This book seeks to answer these questions, and others, by untangling what happened in San Francisco to Food Not Bombs between 1988 and 1995, a period in which they received over 1000 citations and arrests. During this time, the conflict between San Francisco Food Not Bombs and the city opened a fissure in the urban order, which enabled the homeless to become political. The conflict also positioned Food Not Bombs, as well as their sister organization Homes Not Jails, as one of the main defenders of the homeless in San Francisco. In addition, the prefigurative nature of Food Not Bombs, and Homes Not Jails, provides a brief glimpse into an alternative urban politics: an anarchistic politics rooted in mutual aid, solidarity, and direct democracy. A central assumption for this book is that San Francisco Food Not Bombs became a threat to the city due to the economic, political, and social context in which they found themselves, and the creative decisions and tactics the activists employed. This means that the group was not an inherent threat to the urban order, but instead that we need to understand the social, political, and economic context of the time, as well as understand the ways in which activists can jump start a dialectic conflict between city officials and homeless activists. Understanding these contexts provides a window for both scholars and activists to better understand the nature of social change and political contestation in gentrifying urban spaces.

This book is neither a historiography of Food Not Bombs, nor a detailed sociological account of the tactics and inner workings of the San Francisco chapter—as interesting as either of those projects might be. Instead, this book is an act of applied political theory that approaches the conflicts between Food Not Bombs and Homes Not Jails and the governing elite of San Francisco as a unique window into the contested nature of urban politics, homelessness, and public space in a neoliberal era. Applied political theory, at least how I am using it here, differs from more traditional political theory in that it is not primarily concerned with parsing philosophic debates between theorists. Instead applied political theory looks to understand theory as a dialectical exchange between academic work and political reality on the ground. To me the goal of this applied type of theory is to allow it to help us understand otherwise confusing and contradictory experiences in political life, but also to use the experiences in practical politics in order to critically engage and expand our theoretical understandings. In a sense, this project tries to take the actions of activists and government officials seriously, and to take their arguments, ideas, and actions as acceptable forms of political theory argumentation.

In this chapter, I provide a brief introduction to the politics of homelessness by discussing the predominance of "sick talk" in addressing homelessness. In exploring this literature review, I contend that the neoliberalizing of homelessness has shifted the "fault" of homelessness onto the individual, thus pathologizing homelessness and justifying increased criminalization and surveillance. Counter to this view, I present an alternative radical homelessness politics rooted in anarchist political theory and the praxis of Food Not Bombs and the Catholic Workers—an anarchist group formed during the Great Depression that promotes social justice, lives with and supports the homeless, and works tirelessly to end militarism and war. This approach seeks to personalize the homeless, while maintaining a systemic critique of capitalism. I end this chapter with a road map for the coming chapters.

Making the homeless *sick*

During the era of the New Deal, much of the dominant discourse surrounding homelessness and poverty was what Teresa Gowan (2010) calls *system talk*. According to Gowan, system talk in the US was popularized by the Industrial Workers of the World, who, during the 1930s, argued that natural boom-and-bust cycles of capitalism, as well as the capitalist need for a reserve army of workers, explained the rise of homelessness during the Great Depression. In their analysis it was not addiction, mental health, or criminality that created the hobos and tramps of the depression but the system of capitalism itself. A de-radicalized version of this argument became the basis of New Deal and Great Society anti-poverty policies, which attempt to regulate and manage the cycles of capitalism and moderate its negative effects.[1] In short, system talk frames homelessness as being caused by structural problems—from economic globalization to the lack of affordable housing—and therefore seeks to bring about structural changes to fix the system rather than the individual (Gowan, 2010).

Starting in the late 1970s the discourse started to shift as the economic crisis and fallout from Watergate led people to question the validity and effectiveness of the welfare state. In questioning the role of government in regulating the excesses of capitalism, political figures, like Ronald Reagan, made it seem like the free market was better left to regulate itself. By removing government's role in regulating capitalism, structural arguments around issues of homelessness and poverty were undermined and shortly homelessness began being framed as an individual choice, in which able-bodied people choose sloth and alcoholism over employment. Since this shift occurred, homelessness politics has been centered on instituting a strong moral code, banning asocial behaviors, policing those who break laws, gutting social services, and re-empowering churches to be the backbone of the social service industry (Vitale, 2009). Gowan defines this approach to homelessness as sick talk. To Gowan, sick talk consists of any attempt to frame addiction, mental illness, or criminality as primary causes of homelessness. Sick talk has its roots in the late sixteenth-century English Poor Laws, during the enclosure of the English commons, and in late nineteenth- and early twentieth-century poorhouses, which sought to instill within the poor and destitute a religious conviction and Protestant work ethic (Katz, 1996). Sick talk, though, is best expressed through the neoliberal homeless politics that 1990s San Francisco typified.

Neoliberalism refers to a political ideology which contends that free market economic relations create the most efficient and philosophically justifiable outcomes. While often defined as a withering of the welfare state, I contend that neoliberalism can instead be seen as a restructuring of the state in a way that promotes market relations, corporate growth, and economic efficiency (Brenner, 2004; J. R. Hackworth, 2007; Harvey, 2011; Soss, Fording, & Schram, 2011). In this regard, neoliberalism is a process of concealing the state, in which policies intentionally hide the power of state coercion from public view and political debate (Lindsey, 2013). The neoliberalization of homelessness was started during the 1980s with the Reagan administration's push to defund urban governments, localize social services, and develop a partnership between charities and state (Poppendieck, 1999).

San Francisco, a major city, with the largest homeless community by percentage of its population, saw the impacts of neoliberal homeless politics most clearly, and as such this book examines early battles between system and sick talk policies. Below is an overview of the way that neoliberal homeless politics operates; while this literature review examines political developments beyond the period I am studying, this is because the impacts of neoliberal homeless politics did not become clear until they were fully implemented in the early twentieth century.

Bill Clinton expanded on the neoliberal policies of Reagan in his Continuum of Care policy, which sought to develop "comprehensive and long-term approaches that will help homeless people become self-sufficient." As noted by Tony Sparks (2012), Continuum of Care moved homelessness policy further away from New Deal welfare policies of the previous generation by utilizing market-based approaches to address homelessness. Sparks writes that,

> Continuum of Care operated upon the assumption that homelessness was the result of a personal failing. Responding to concerns by both liberal homeless advocates and conservative critics, the program reflected a growing consensus that simple shelter provisions did little to help the homeless . . . the effect was the simultaneous normalization and personalization of homelessness. No longer was homelessness a product of economic crisis requiring emergency response. Rather the appropriate remedy was the rehabilitation and training of the homeless individual to the norms of entrepreneurial individualism for a personal problem. (Sparks, 2012: 1516)

Not surprisingly, the George W. Bush administration continued this project by expanding the usage of market-based assessments of homelessness services, looking to make social services as efficient and business-like as possible. The impact of this market-based approach, when combined with his administration's policies on chronic homelessness, led to a further pathologizing of homelessness. Vincent Del Casino and Christine Jocoy (2008), in discussing Bush's policies, noted: "The chronic are neither autonomous, responsible citizens, nor effective, productive neoliberal subjects" (Del Casino & Jocoy, 2008: 194). This effectively marks the homeless and poor as being unable to take care of themselves and as being economically unfit, and therefore justifies increased paternalistic policies by the federal government. By positioning the homeless and chronically poor in this light, their poverty is the result of their individual actions and individual failings. These policies had the impact of pushing service providers towards making alcohol, drug, and mental health services the centerpieces of their homeless policies. The common wisdom that the rise in homelessness during the 1980s was caused by deinstitutionalization—the release of mental health patients into the community due to mental hospital closures—was actually not the case, and in fact, states like California actually saw a small increase in mental hospital residents during the period. If anything, the period between 1950 and 1975 saw the largest wave of deinstitutionalization, while at the same time no noticeable rise in homelessness occurred (National Coalition for the Homeless, 2006). While cuts to mental services health most likely compounded the problem of homelessness, I would contend that homelessness is primarily connected to poverty and a weak social safety net. In other words, homelessness is a symptom of capitalism's excesses. This claim is supported by broader work of the National Coalition for the Homeless, which has regularly argued that their data show that mental health is not the primary cause of homelessness, and that the focus on mental health and addiction services, while occasionally important, can also distract us from the structural causes of homelessness, i.e., extreme poverty and the gutting of the social welfare state (National Coalition for the Homeless, n.d., 2006, 2007).

By pathologizing the homeless and analyzing their success through market-based outcomes, neoliberal policies have expanded dragnet surveillance as well. Tony Sparks (2010) highlights the surveillance programs associated with neoliberalism in his article "Broke Not Broken: Rights, Privacy, and Homelessness in Seattle." In this article, Sparks discusses homeless opposition to a citywide homeless registration system, called Safe Harbors HMIS, meant to cut fraud and abuse and better monitor how well homeless residents are responding to the city's treatment programs. This program not only monitored and regulated the homeless, but reinforced the sick talk discourse of homelessness by centering data collection at alcohol and drug treatment centers, mental health service providers, and city shelter systems (Sparks, 2010).

Stacey Murphy details the government policies impacting homeless residents of San Francisco in the supposedly humane politics of Gavin Newsom's San Francisco. Currently in San Francisco, there are a few thousand city-funded, privately owned Single Room Occupancy (SRO) hotels that homeless residents are forced to pay for with over $300 of their $365 General Assistance (GA) fund money. Access to city funded beds is limited; when not available, homeless residents are instead given month-long stays in emergency shelters on a first come first served basis. By further limiting the SRO stock and emergency shelter spacing it has become significantly harder for homeless individuals to exist outside the program, as those unwilling, or unable, to go through what is known as the "care not cash" program are forced to go from shelter to shelter hoping to get a night or week-long stay (Murphy, 2009).

The city thus coerces the homeless to either give up the majority of their GA benefits to access an SRO room, many of which fail to meet basic housing codes, or to risk harassment and violence by sleeping on the street or in a park. If the homeless accept the program, they are then required to: go through budgeting classes which help them budget the remaining $65 dollars a month they have to live on; apply for jobs on a regular basis; and accept a handful of overt surveillance programs in the SRO, including room searches, having to sign in every time they enter or leave, not being allowed to have any guests in their rooms without a manager's permission, and being under constant surveillance via closed circuit cameras. If they fail to live up to any of these requirements, they lose their housing and are banned from the program for an entire year.

These neoliberal institutions are designed to promote disciplinary control over the homeless and poor, making them jump through hoops and follow arbitrary rules in order to get needed service. Working through the charity system requires that one learn to accept and follow the demands of the *authority*, be it welfare agent, soup kitchen employees, shelter monitors, or hotel managers. The neoliberalization of homelessness services does not lead to the personalizing of the homeless, even though it does individualize the causes of homelessness. Instead, it provides a new method for governing and regulating homeless bodies. By constructing the homeless community as a population, market approaches and techniques can be used for the benefit of those in power. In this regard, the neoliberal conception of homelessness has not advanced much from the constructing and disciplining of the delinquent described by Foucault: "The establishment of a delinquency that constitutes something like an enclosed illegality has in fact a number of advantages. To begin with, it is possible to supervise it" (Foucault, 1995: 278). This process requires defining delinquency around concepts of illegality, addiction, and moral failing, which is exactly what neoliberalism has done to the homeless. By doing this, as Foucault mentions, it makes the homeless a manageable population. The reason for this, according to Jeff Ferrell is that: "They [the ruling elite] embody a vision of streets swept free of marginalized populations, cleared of human trash and the uncomfortable reminder of social decay they present—an urban environment made safe for endless, effortless consumption, for the discovery of plastic-wrapped urban charm and prepackaged urban adventure" (Ferrell, 2001: 15).

Current homelessness policies do not embrace the complex value and identities found within homeless individuals, but work to turn that person into a statistic, into one more piece of population data. In constructing the archetype of homeless individuals, this process seeks to pathologize the homeless—searching for the individual causes of the symptom—and then requires a system of surveillance and management to regulate the homeless population. The goal for neoliberal homeless policies is not to empower the homeless or even to get them permanently off the streets, even if that occasionally does happen, but to construct docile and controllable bodies.

Turning statistics into people: anarchism, personalism, and radical systems talk

While the neoliberal model of homelessness largely seeks to manage and control the homeless community, the radical homeless politics that develops out of Food Not Bombs, Homes Not Jails, the Catholic Workers and many others, rejects managed order for the chaotic, fun, and playful examples found in homeless tent-cities, free forming busker concerts, and graffiti art. By embracing the figure of the lumpenproletariat as a class fighting against the order of bourgeois society, Food Not Bombs taps into a long anarchist history.

The lumpenproletariat was defined by Marx in *The 18th Brumaire of Louis Napoleon* thus:

> Alongside decayed roués with dubious means of subsistence and of dubious origin, alongside ruined and adventurous offshoots of the bourgeoisie, were vagabonds, discharged soldiers, discharged jailbirds, escaped galley slaves, swindlers, mountebanks, lazzaroni, pickpockets, tricksters, gamblers, maquereaux [pimps], brothel keepers, porters, literati, organ grinders, ragpickers, knife grinders, tinkers, beggars—in short, the whole indefinite, disintegrated mass, thrown hither and thither, which the French call *la bohème*. (Marx, 1852)

This class of beggars, drug users, prostitutes and gutter dwellers served as a reactionary force to Marx. To him, the lumpenproletariat were easily bought and manipulated by elites and therefore lacked the radical potential of the working classes.

Unlike Marxism, anarchism—starting with Bakunin, who Engels dubbed the "Lumpen King"—embraced the lumpenproletariet as being a radical class. As Nocholas Thoburn writes:

> Bakunin considers workers' integration in capital as destructive of more primary revolutionary forces. For Bakunin, the revolutionary archetype is found in a peasant milieu (which is presented as having longstanding insurrectionary traditions, as well as a communist archetype in its current social form—the peasant commune) and amongst educated unemployed youth, assorted marginals from all classes, brigands, robbers, the impoverished masses, and those on the margins of society who have escaped, been excluded from, or not yet subsumed in "the discipline of emerging industrial work"—in short, all those whom Marx sought to include in the category of the lumpenproletariat. (Thoburn, 2002: 445)

To Bakunin, the underclass of capitalism has a revolutionary potential that is actually much greater than that of the working class, because they have nothing else to lose. This is a similar argument to the anti-workerist tendencies in anarchism—from Hakim Bay (2003) and Bob Black (1986) to the Situationists (Wark, 2013, 2015)—which position work as a domesticating process that turns workers into reactionary actors. The orthodox Marxist view focuses exclusively on paid wage labor and therefore ignores the work of women in the domestic sphere and the work that urban scavengers engage in to survive. The revolutionary potential of the lumpenproletariat can be seen in their influential role in medieval bread riots, urban and workplace strikes, and in the development of civil rights during the 1960s (Hobsbawm, 1996; Piven, 2006). Likewise, according to Thaddeus Russell (2011), figures like prostitutes, drag queens, and drug users have played central roles in the expansion of democratic and civil rights throughout much of US history, being central to the development of revolutionary fervor in cities like Philadelphia before the war for independence and in the construction of women's rights in the Western Territories.

The homeless are also uniquely positioned to highlight certain aspects of capitalist economics and state policies. This is because the homeless, unlike the industrial workers, are the most economically marginalized members of a society, and as such provide a contrast to highlight income inequality, the inhumane nature of capitalist economic relations, and the paternalistic and insulting nature of state social service institutions. They also, according to Leonard Feldman (2006) and Kathleen Arnold (2004), serve as an other that is used to justify the liberal conceptions of citizenship; as the normative citizen is often defined in contrast to the image of the irrational, lazy, and broken lumpenproletariat. As an excluded economic and political figure, the homeless when empowered and politicized have the ability to alter contemporary political arrangements. A radical homeless politics thus understands the unique positionality and transformative potential of homeless politics.

Unlike Marxists and liberal theorists, who look at the lumpenproletariat with disdain, anarchistic movements have commonly looked to them for inspiration, motivation, rage, and action. Kropotkin (2011), for instance, saw the poor as engaging in the practice of mutual aid in order to survive; while Jeff Ferrell (2001) sees homeless squatters, street punks, graffiti artists, and bored youth as the vanguard of liberated public space. Thus through their "geographies of survival" (Mitchell & Heynen, 2009) the homeless and poor keep the practices of mutual aid alive during periods of selfishness and greed. In this regard, they are both victims of capitalist economic relations and an important locus of class struggle.

What makes the radical homelessness politics of groups like Food Not Bombs and the Catholic Workers unique is not that they embrace a systems talk, but that they fuse systems talk with radical *personalism*. Personalism, which has its roots in Catholic theology and the writings of Thoreau and Tolstoy, is a European religious ethical philosophy developed by Emmanuel Mounier. To Mounier, each and every person was modeled in the image of

1.3 Soupstock performance, 2000

God and therefore was uniquely beautiful and valuable. Therefore no person is worth more than another and no person is expendable (McKanan, 2008). As such Mournier and his Catholic Worker followers hold a deep skepticism of central state agencies and charities, both of which are cold, impersonal, and bureaucratic (McKanan, 2008: 9). For Dorothy Day and the Catholic Workers, personalism was further radicalized through its connection with prefigurative politics and radical social justice. To Dorothy Day, welfare state institutions are antithetical to personalism, as those institutions serve as mediator between people and works of compassion (McKanan, 2008; Sniegocki, 2005). This connection between ethical personalism and unmediated politics can be seen in the "Aims and Means" of the Catholic Workers, which states, "We move away from a self-centered individualism towards the good of the other. This is to be done by taking personal responsibility for changing conditions, rather than looking to the state or to other institutions to provide impersonal charity" (Catholic Worker Movement, n.d.).

While that statement can be seen as potentially paternalistic, with its benevolent concern for the other, the ideal of precarity and voluntary poverty promoted by Day theoretically works to help break down any hierarchies and barriers between Catholic Workers and the homeless. Day wrote, "Through voluntary poverty we will have the means to help our brothers. We cannot even see our brothers in need without first stripping ourselves. It is the only way we have of showing our love" (D. Day, 1981: 109). In short, according to Day, one should accept a life of poverty, precarity, and constant questioning of privilege in order to show one's solidarity and love with the homeless and poor. Such practices would allow one to understand their plight and to be unshackled by fear of state persecution in order to limit any privileges that Catholic Workers might otherwise have.

While personalism, in my analysis, is central to understanding radical homelessness politics, the Catholic Worker version of it often relies too heavily on a politics of sacrifice. In fact, the personalism of Maurin and Day is rooted in the belief that, in order to follow the model of Jesus, Catholic Workers should sacrifice in order to help those in need. This politics of self-sacrifice and martyrdom should be criticized, especially since personalism does not require it. Benjamin Shepard, the Situationists, and the post-left anarchists often highlight the many ways that play, fun, and revelry help create radical spaces (Shepard & Smithsimon, 2011); in this regard radical politics, while personalist and serious, is not centered on sacrifice but play.

In my own experiences with Food Not Bombs, ours was not a politics of sacrifice and martyrdom, even though we mostly all wore black. Often, though not often enough, people would play music, tell stories, or engage in art projects that enlivened our meals. Even the few times that I had the pleasure of hanging out with people at their homeless encampments, the mood was not always solemn, in fact it was often more of a celebration, reminding us that homeless encampments are not always (if ever) the bare-life camps described by Agamben (Agamben, 1998, 2005). Likewise, many of the stories told to me by current and former members of San Francisco Food Not Bombs are tales that combine political activism and humor. In one such story, an activist told me what happened when he jumped into a fountain in front of City Hall with a pot of soup, to avoid being arrested by the police. The water fight, laughter, and arrests that followed serve as a powerful reminder that people often engage in radical activism because they have fun doing so. This all said, the concept of personalism allows for these groups to provide respect and love for individuals while acknowledging and working against oppressive and destructive institutions. It also provides the foundation for a deep politics of solidarity and affinity to develop between the homeless and non-homeless activists in groups like Food Not Bombs.

What emerges then, in radical homelessness politics, is a personalized *systems talk* which understands that the capitalist economic system and state policies work in tandem to construct a world in which poverty and precarity are all too common. Unlike neoliberal response to homelessness, which seeks to pathologize and criminalize the homeless, the radical homelessness politics that will be described throughout this book seeks to engage in a politics of empowerment and solidarity. The concern is not finding

efficient ways to alleviate the negative consequences of homelessness, but
to treat homeless individuals as people, to build close relationships with
them, to show them care, friendship and support no matter how time-
consuming and inefficient this process may be. The aim for radical homeless
politics is to create a politics that empowers those who are disempowered
under the current system. This empowered politics must be mutually constitutive and be a politics of solidarity, not one rooted in the logic of burden
and sacrifice in which those with privilege liberate the other. Peter Kropotkin, in advocating for prison abolition, highlights what this solidaristic
politics might look like. He writes:

> What prisoners have not found today in society is a helping hand, simple
> and friendly, which would aid them from childhood to develop the higher
> faculties of their mind and souls . . . But these superior faculties of the
> mind and heart cannot be exercised by a person deprived of liberty, if
> he never has much of a choice . . . Human fraternity and liberty are the
> only correctives to apply to those diseases of the human organism which
> lead to so called crime. (Kropotkin, 1975: 233)

He contends that through abolishing prisons, redistributing wealth and
housing, and the development of self-empowered communities, we can
humanely and respectfully address the issue of crime. The same applies to
homelessness.

One of the defining characteristics of radical homeless politics, as I see
it, is an aversion to moralizing and judging the homeless. In the case of the
Catholic Workers, this was typified by the personal practices of Day, who
while a critic of abortion rights and homosexuality, never imposed her views
on others or tried to fix someone or convert them. Likewise, the Catholic
Workers were known for showing as much love and openness to those with
addiction problems as those without because, drunk or not, people deserve
to be treated as human beings and shown respect. This differs drastically
from religious and secular shelters and soup kitchens, which commonly
have rules against such behavior. The acceptance of people as they are, by
groups like Food Not Bombs and the Catholic Workers, allows for the
radical homeless movement to acknowledge that while living on the streets
is often the result of coercive structural violence, it can also be a choice,
one that is neither morally wrong nor irrational. In fact, in my years
working with Food Not Bombs I have met many people who, either because
of bad circumstances or an unwillingness to engage in the rat race, decided
to live on the streets. Unlike missions and state social services, groups like
Food Not Bombs do not place moral judgment on such decisions and, if
anything, actively support such practices, seeing voluntary homelessness as
a form of political resistance.

The radical homelessness politics discussed in this book is rather complex. Groups like Food Not Bombs are openly hostile to capitalism and see the commodification of food and housing as being a form of violence perpetrated on the poor, as we will see in more detail in the next chapter. This systemic analysis is combined with a deep commitment to respect and care for individuals. The politics that develops here understands and acknowledges that the homeless are both victims of capitalism and political actors making decisions. As such, radical homeless politics is not predicated on fixing the homeless, or moralizing and pathologizing homelessness, addiction, citizenship, or other geographies of survival. Instead, a radical homeless politics seeks to fight against the structural institutions that commit violence against the poor, while empowering the poor to be autonomous political actors. To put it another way, the goal is not to get all homeless out of tent-cities and off the streets but to create a world where all can live, survive, and make the decisions that they think is best for them—even if that means living on the streets.

Our path from here

The rest of this book will examine homeless resistance to neoliberal homelessness policies in San Francisco between 1988 and 1995, in order to highlight the contested nature of space, economics, and politics. During this period a progressive and a conservative democratic mayor both waged city-wide campaigns to address the issue of homelessness. In both cases, the city policies were about hiding or erasing the homeless from the urban environment and not about empowering them. It was because of this that Food Not Bombs became such an important and powerful political force in the city. This popularity came about not only because the group was exceptional at publicizing their actions and framing the debate around homelessness, but because the group's radical homeless politics stood in stark contrast to the dehumanizing policies of the city. In a city like San Francisco, with a long history of radical activism, their action tapped into a vein of popular support that allowed the group material, political, and social resources that were never available in other cities.

Chapter 2 provides an introduction to Food Not Bombs by providing a brief history of the group, from their involvement in the anti-nuke movement in Boston to their role in providing disaster relief after hurricane Katrina. This history shows the group's strong connection to a large range of movements, and contextualizes San Francisco Food Not Bombs and its role in the rapid expansion of Food Not Bombs, which now has around 1000 chapters worldwide. Finally, this chapter provides an analysis of

Food Not Bombs' political project. While figures like Howard Zinn have stated that Food Not Bombs' politics are simple and straightforward—fight militarism and feed people—I contend that their political project is much more nuanced and complex. I contend that the Food Not Bombs project has three components to it: (1) a complex understanding of non-violence; (2) an anarchistic critique of private charity and the state; and (3) an adherence to prefigurative politics. By combining these concepts, Food Not Bombs provides a unique political project that will be taken up further in chapter 6.

Chapter 3 uses the struggle between Food Not Bombs and the Art Agnos mayoral administration (1988–1991) as a backdrop to discuss the role of permits in regulating and controlling space. I contend that Food Not Bombs, through public feedings and organizing tent-cities, made specific claims regarding the nature of public space and argued that the city had no legitimacy to regulate political activism and expression. The city, on the other hand, attempted to use permits as means of forcing the group into a negotiated management with city officials. When that negotiation broke down, the city turned toward an escalation of violence and harassment in an attempt to purge the group from public space. In considering anarchist and autonomous conceptions of public space, I expand on Margaret Kohn's conception of populist *space* (2003, 2013) by exploring how autonomous politics complicates the topic. In contrast, I contend that a complex dialectical relationship exists between the autonomous populist politics of Food Not Bombs, the populist representational nature of public protest, and the regulatory desire of the city.

Chapter 4 discusses mayor Frank Jordan's (1992–1995) revanchist Matrix Quality of Life Program, which sought to enforce a broken-windows policing system in San Francisco. The impact of the policy was felt largely by the visible homeless in downtown San Francisco, who were regularly harassed and arrested by the police and forced out of the city. Because quality-of-life policing desires to sanitize the public space of disruptive and asocial behaviour, the public meals of Food Not Bombs near City Hall resisted the city's attempt to criminalize homelessness. In this chapter, I argue that the city attempted to construct the homeless as anti-citizens and exclude them from the political and physical spaces of the city.

In chapter 5, I turn to the activism and politics of anarchist homeless activists in resisting the cities' attempts to exclude the homeless. I turn to two important political theorists to make sense of the resistance of Food Not Bombs: Jacques Rancière and Eduard Glissant. Rancière's short piece "Ten theses on politics" provides a powerful understanding of the way that disruptive actions and resistance expand political space, while Glissant's idea of right to opacity examines the complex relationship of violence, power, and visibility. I argue that the homeless have a right to opacity from the state, and state surveillance, and that the homeless should only be as visible as they want to be. This means that public occupations, political protests, and public meals are legitimate forms of visibility, which respect homeless people's right to be opaque, while programs such as San Francisco's Matrix plan are a coercive form of violence.

In chapter 6 we look at the response from the Jordan administration on Food Not Bombs' sister organization, Homes Not Jails, which illegally housed the homeless in abandoned buildings. In interviews with people involved in both Food Not Bombs and Homes Not Jails, I was often told stories of police leniency with the squatters, something that was unheard of for Food Not Bombs' actions. This differential treatment has to do with the political nature of space and the city's desire to hide the homeless from public view. Because the city wanted to push the homeless into private space, I conclude that Homes Not Jails, by illegally housing the homeless in abandoned houses, ended up unintentionally working to help the Jordan administration achieve part of this public space goal. This chapter argues that city agencies react to autonomous political projects differently depending on whether they erupt in what the state defines as public or private space.

In the last full chapter, I put the lessons from the anarchist urban activism and praxis of Food Not Bombs and Homes Not Jails into dialogue with the work on the right to the city. While I am sympathetic and inspired by these theorists' work on radical urbanism, I criticize productionist predilections and highlight that centralized homelessness removes the focus on formal economic production. I also contend that by focusing on the homeless, a more robust and radical conception of urban space as commons can be developed, which allows for rights to opacity and survival in urban space.

Notes

1   The disciplinary nature of New Deal social welfare programs was well documented by Francis Fox Piven and Richard Cloward in their groundbreaking book *Regulating the Poor*, which argued that social service bureaucracies serve the interests of economic and political elites. As such, these institutions are structured not to empower and help the poor, but to regulate and manage them (Piven & Cloward, 1993). This work and others by Piven and Cloward provide a much needed critique of the New Deal and Great Society social welfare programs and argue for poor people to embrace disruptive protest as a means of expanding social service provisions and reforming the institution (Piven & Cloward, 1979).

2

What dumpstered soup tells us about violence, charity, and politics

They don't want to feed the hungry, they just want to make an anarchist type statement and we aren't going to allow it. (Former San Francisco Police Captain Dennis Martel)

They feel they can manipulate the homeless issue to set the stage for some kind of radical new order. (Former San Francisco mayor Art Agnos)

"I love the smell of a full dumpster" is a phrase I hope no one has ever said. For those people who have never gone dumpstering, I can honestly tell you, the smell can be alarming. At most grocery stores the dumpster is filled with a cornucopia of fresh produce, rotting food, and basic garbage. The combo of the three, with the right amount of sunlight, rain, and time can knock you off your feet. But the treasure trove of edible produce can turn even the biggest germaphobe into a partisan dumpster diver. I have grabbed box after box of fresh organic produce—from artichoke hearts, apples, potatoes, and onions, to dragon fruit and mangos—and a wild assortment of pasta sauces, chocolate bars, and fake meat. Most of this food was thrown out, not because it was no longer edible, but because it was either blemished or bruised or because it had just reached its sell-by date. This is especially problematic since the amount that goes to waste in the United States is astronomical. According to an NPR report, in 2010, 31% of the total food produced in the country was thrown away and 19% of all the fruit and vegetables harvested by exploited migrant farmers rotted away in a landfill or dumpster behind a store (Barclay, 2014). Meanwhile, in 2013, 49 million Americans, or 1 in 6 of the people living within the borders of the United States, faced food insecurity ("11 Facts About Hunger in the US | DoSomething.org | Volunteer for Social Change," n.d.).

While millions of people in the United States go to sleep hungry, the legal system has made it a crime to glean thrown away food from garbage cans since the contents of the dumpsters are the property of the trash companies that own them, and explorations into the dark depths of the receptacle by activists, the homeless, or the hungry is not only trespassing but theft. You can be arrested for stealing garbage from a supermarket dumpster, yet no one is ever arrested for keeping edible food away from the 50 million hungry people who would love to eat it.

Food Not Bombs looks to both attack and highlight the gross absurdity of our food waste. The group, by taking waste produce and turning it into healthy food for hungry people, not only addresses the problem of hunger but also informs the community about the amount of food being wasted. Sometimes these adventures for food are fun as well. On one uniquely humorous occasion, a friend and I biked through the night across the Franklin Street bridge to explore what treasures awaited us at the Eugene Trader Joe's, located in the corner of a large strip mall. The dumpster, emblazoned with the green and blue logo of the local waste company SANIPAC, is behind the store, protected from the general public by a 6-foot tall chain link fence. On this lucky occasion the fence was unlocked and we were able to hop in. We found a huge assortment of great Trader Joe's fare, from jars of organic peanut butter, to bars and bars of dark chocolate. While we were filling our bags with all the goodies we could, the local security guard heard our joyful laughing and saw our flickering headlamps, and with my friend waist deep into the dumpster rummaging for a package of apples, we heard from a distance "STOP! STOP! WHAT ARE YOU TWO DOING? YOU ARE STEALING FROM SANIPAC!" His anger exemplifies the problem of how the priorities of our society are upside down. Instead of expressing anger at a system that allows tens of millions to go to bed with empty stomachs, this man's anger was directed at two mid-twenty-year-olds grabbing chocolate bars destined to rot in landfill.

Food Not Bombs helps to create a counter narrative around food, hunger, poverty, and capitalism. Instead of being angry at theft from a dumpster, Food Not Bombs calls us to express our rage against an economic, political, and legal system that criminalizes being poor and valorizes that which creates poverty in the first place. In this chapter, I provide a brief history of Food Not Bombs, paying special attention to the role of San Francisco Food Not Bombs in the growth and development of the movement. In addition to providing a quick historical background on the movement, this chapter will also serve to untangle and discuss Food Not Bombs' political project. I contend that the group's politics is more complicated than the banners and slogans the group uses. The group's mission is about more than stopping war and providing free food—it is about understanding the complex intersections of violence and oppression, and building alternative, life-affirming institutions to counter the culture of death that plagues modern life under capitalism.

Feeding the revolution? A short history of Food Not Bombs

Food Not Bombs formed out of the anti-nuclear movement of the 1980s, when activists from the Coalition for Direct Action at Seabrook in New England organized a bake sale to raise legal funds for Brian Feigenbaum, an activist charged with assaulting an officer during a protest on May 24, 1980. The activists dressed as generals and sold pastries on Boston streets with a banner that read "I'm waiting for the day when schools get all the money they need and the Air Force has to hold a bake sale for a bomber" (Butler & McHenry, 2000). After Brian's release, the group organized a mock 1930s-style soup kitchen during a shareholders' meeting of the First National Bank of Boston, one of the banks involved in funding the controversial Seabrook nuclear power plant. The mock soup kitchen became a real soup kitchen when at least fifty homeless and hungry people stopped by to eat and protest (Butler & McHenry, 2000).

Following the shareholders' action, members of the group began squatting in a house on Harvard Street and soliciting food donations from health food stores. The group collected distressed food daily and provided it to Rose's Place—a shelter for battered women—as well as to drug rehab clinics, homeless service groups, immigrant rights organizations, and other progressive and left-wing service providers. In addition, every Monday in Harvard Square, they would provide a vegan meal for all who were hungry, while also distributing literature about military interventions, nuclear weapons, and social and military policy (figure 1.3) (Butler & McHenry, 2000).

While maintaining their involvement within the anti-nuclear movement, Food Not Bombs activists during this period were also involved in the east coast peace movement. It was this interaction between Food Not Bombs and the anti-nuke movement that helped redefine contemporary American anarchism. Within the anti-nuke movements, anarchist politics merged with the praxis and politics of radical Quakers, leading to the development of a strongly democratic and prefigurative politics, which as we shall see, became central to the politics of Food Not Bombs (Epstein, 1991). In working with the east coast anti-nuke movement, the group helped organize both the June 12, 1982, "March for Nuclear Disarmament" in New York City, and the "Free Concert for Nuclear Disarmament" in May of 1982 in Boston. They worked closely with the Cambridge City Hall in organizing anti-nuclear days of action in conjunction with the anniversary of the bombings of Hiroshima and Nagasaki. They were even active enough that Abbey Hoffman put Food Not Bombs into his book, *Steal this pee-test*, regarding their Boston "Pee Party" protest against the escalation of the War on Drugs and its impact on the poor.[1] Food Not Bombs even disrupted America's favorite pastime by protesting the city's mistreatment of the homeless by distributing free food in front of Fenway Park during the 1986 Major League Baseball playoffs (Butler & McHenry, 2000).

San Francisco Food Not Bombs had its start in late 1987, shortly after co-founder Keith McHenry moved to the city. McHenry and others began serving food on the corner of Haight and Stanton, near the edge of Golden Gate Park. On August 15, 1988, the city of San Francisco arrested 15 people from Food Not Bombs for distributing food without a permit, marking the first time in the movement's entire history that this happened. These arrests ended up being the start of an eight-year battle between the city of San Francisco and the group. During this conflict, which spanned two mayoral administrations, over 1000 activists were cited or arrested for distributing food without a permit, violating a court injunction, or resisting arrest.

The media coverage of the arrests, police harassment, and the publication of *The Food Not Bombs Menu* made the San Francisco chapter central to the massive expansion of Food Not Bombs' movement. Embracing its role, the San Francisco chapter organized the 1992 first National Food Not Bombs gathering, with approximately 75 people in attendance, representing nearly all of the 30 chapters that existed at the time (McHenry, 2012: 103). During this gathering, activists from around the country discussed the politics of Food Not Bombs and developed the guiding principles for the group, which are:

1. The food is always vegan or vegetarian and free to everyone without restriction, rich or poor, stoned or sober
2. Food Not Bombs has no formal leaders or headquarters, and every group is autonomous and makes decisions using the consensus process
3. Food Not Bombs is dedicated to non-violent direct action and works for non-violent social change (McHenry, 2012: 17).

These guiding principles, as well as the publication of the first edition of the organization's book, *Food Not Bombs*, in 1992 provided much needed outreach for the growing movement.

Three years after the first gathering, the San Francisco chapter organized an international gathering to coincide with the 50th anniversary of the United Nations. The ten days of workshops, protests, tent-cities, and street theatre will be discussed in detail in chapter 4, but this second gathering shows the rapid growth of the movement. While the first gathering, just two years prior, had only 75 people in attendance, in 1994 over 600 people participated in the gathering, representing chapters from the US, Canada, Mexico, and Europe (McHenry, 2012: 106).

The harassment got so bad that following the 1994 gathering and tent-city protest of the United Nations 50th anniversary celebration, Amnesty International threatened to designate Food Not Bombs activists as

"Prisoners of Consciousness." In their letter to the city, Amnesty International wrote:

> Amnesty International is concerned that the Food Not Bombs activists may have been targeted on account of their beliefs and effectively prohibited from exercising their right to freedom of expression, assembly, and the right to impart information. If this were found to be the case, the City of San Francisco would be in breach of international law and Amnesty International would adopt those imprisoned as "Prisoners of Conscience" and work for their unconditional release. (Amnesty International, 1994)

During the 1990s, Food Not Bombs began connecting its opposition to militarism, capitalism, and ecocide with resistance to the newly minted Free Trade agreements. During this time, Food Not Bombs' meals became commonplace at anti-WTO protests throughout the world; in 1999, Food Not Bombs chapters throughout the nation worked together to coordinate food services for the WTO protest in Seattle. From the mid-1990s on, Food Not Bombs has been involved in nearly every major left-wing protest in North America, from the massive protests opposing the Wars in Iraq and Afghanistan, to the public occupations of parks during Occupy Wall Street. In fact, any person who has been to a major protest in the last few decades has seen the groups' icon image (figure 2.1) and many have even eaten a meal cooked in a Food Not Bombs kitchen. The group's involvement at different protests also helped connect Food Not Bombs to other political movements—from animal and earth liberation, to prison abolitionism, to immigrant rights, and feminism. The wide-ranging roots of resistance that Food Not Bombs has watered have been referred to by Richard Day as typifying the politics of groundless solidarity (R. J. F. Day, 2005). In practice, one can see Food Not Bombs as the catering wing of the US radical left.

While Food Not Bombs was becoming part of the global protest movement, it was also cementing itself as one of the most successful disaster relief organizations in the United States. In 1989, San Francisco Food Not Bombs was one of the first organizations to provide food after the October 17 6.9-magnitude earthquake that hit the city. Many of the activists I interviewed from San Francisco Food Not Bombs argued that the group's actions following the earthquake were a reason that Art Agnos backed off arresting Food Not Bombs activists during the second half of his term as mayor. Food Not Bombs activists have also been at the forefront in relief after the September 11 terrorist attacks in New York City and after the devastation of New Orleans after Hurricane Katrina in 2005. In the case of Katrina, organizers from Hartford, Connecticut coordinated with 20 other chapters to create a community food relief center in the 9th ward of New Orleans

2.1 Food Not Bombs logo

a week after the hurricane. The activists from Food Not Bombs in New Orleans were also involved in the development of Common Ground, a New Orleans radical community center that provides food, clothing, medical, legal, and other services for the community. Finally, Food Not Bombs, in coordination with the Occupy movement, was one of the first organizations to set up relief programs in New York following Hurricane Sandy in 2012. At one event in Long Island, coordinated by Food Not Bombs and Occupy Sandy, over 100 people showed up in the aftermath of the hurricane to receive free food, clothes, and other much-needed survival items.

During the 1990s, Food Not Bombs also became associated with contemporary anarchism, and are now one of the most recognizable anarchist groups in the world. While originally the group was not explicitly anarchist, these tendencies thrived during their early years, partially because of the influence and importance of anarchist principles within the anti-nuke movement they developed out of (Epstein, 1991). The San Francisco chapter, which had large numbers of anarchist organizers, as well as strong connections with the underground punk scene in the Bay area, helped develop the connection between Food Not Bombs and anarchism. Chris Crass, a San Francisco Food Not Bombs organizer from 1993–2000, most succinctly highlighted the connection between the group and anarchism in his short

Stop Violence
Against Clinics
Come Protest the
recent bombings

This
Sunday

Jan.
26
1801 Bush St.

APRIL 20. 1920
MY MOTHER DIED
OF AN
ILLEGAL ABORTION

Stand Up
for Women's
Reproductive
Rights at
a Health
Clinic.

10:00AM at Bush
and Octavia
Speak Out ▲ March ▲ Action
Bay Area Coalition On Reproductive Rights •Refuse and Resist• Women's Choice Clinic

2.2 Flier for Reproductive Rights Coalition, which Food Not Bombs was a part of

but influential article "Non-Violence and Anarchism." In this article Crass writes:

Anarchism is movement for a society in which the violence of racism, sexism, homophobia, capitalism, and coercion are removed from our daily lives. Anarchism is the belief in a world without war and economic poverty. Anarchism is a philosophy and movement working to build cooperative, egalitarian human relationships and social structures that promote mutual aid, radical democratic control of political and economic decisions, and ecological sustainability. So how does this apply directly to FNB? (Crass, 1995)

In answering the question that underlies this article, Crass argues that the principles of Food Not Bombs (non-violence, animal rights, consensus, and direct action) are all explicitly anarchist principles. He asserts that even though anarchism is often misunderstood in public debates, the group should explicitly view itself as part of this wider movement. The article was widely circulated and has become influential in Food Not Bombs and anarchist circles.

Due to the group's personalist politics and chapter autonomy, any overview of the group's history inherently misses the multifaceted experiences of countless activists and their relationships and interactions with homeless communities. The occasional conflicts that flare up between Food Not Bombs activists and city officials garner much of the news coverage, but the daily actions and experiences are essential to what Food Not Bombs was, what the group is, and what it will become. Some of these experiences are exciting, such as the experience of activists who traveled down to the flooded streets of the 9th Ward in New Orleans, following Hurricane Katrina, to help form the radical community space, Common Ground. Other stories were quietly revelatory, such as my experiences eating and talking to homeless veterans, bohemian poets, and even a former college professor turned nomadic work refuser. These daily stories of Food Not Bombs gleaners, cooks, servers, and noshers are where social justice, direct action, and anarchism combine to create a political movement. It is the quiet meals, where no one is arrested, that offer a glimpse into what our emancipated future might look like.

The politics of dumpstered food

Howard Zinn, in describing Food Not Bombs, wrote "the message of Food Not Bombs is simple and powerful: no one should be without food in a world so richly provided with land, sun, and human ingenuity. No consideration of money, no demand for profit, should stand in the way of any hungry or malnourished child or any adult in need." In addition he said, "This slogan requires no complicated analysis. Those three words say it all. They point unerringly to the double challenge: to immediately feed people who are without adequate food, and to replace a system whose priorities are power and profit with one meeting the needs of all human beings" (Zinn, 2000). Likewise, Keith McHenry in *Hungry for peace*, correctly states that "The name Food Not Bombs states our most fundamental principle: society

needs to promote life, not death. Implement the positive and end cooperation with the negative. Live in a world of abundance and stop fearing a
future of scarcity. Celebrate with love not hate; cooperation instead of
domination and compassion, not exploitation" (McHenry, 2012: 17). What
McHenry shows is that while Zinn is correct in asserting that the group's
name highlights the simplicity of their message, the politics that emerge
from that message are rather complex. In other words, while the group's
slogan is simple, their politics are not. I contend there are three principles
which Food Not Bombs has developed over their 30 years of political action
that are central to Food Not Bombs' politics. They are: (1) food should not
be a weapon; (2) solidarity not charity; (3) build a new world in the shell
of the old.

Food should not be a weapon

Food Not Bombs, as discussed above, emerged out of the peace and anti-
nuclear movement and has always identified itself as part of the non-
violence movement. In embracing non-violence, Food Not Bombs has
constantly contrasted its non-violent politics with the institutional and
structural violence of neoliberalism and austerity politics. As co-founders
Keith McHenry and C. T. Butler stated:

> Globally, we continue to spend more time and resources developing,
> using, and threatening to use weapons of massive human and planetary
> destruction than on nurturing and celebrating life. By spending this
> money on bombs instead of food, our government perpetuates and exac-
> erbates poverty's violence by not providing food for everyone in need.
> (Butler & McHenry, 2000: 72)

As this quote shows, Food Not Bombs understands poverty as a form of
structural violence; while the violence of poverty is not as spectacular as
bombs and bullets, it is just as horrific in its impact, thus poverty, hunger,
and gentrification are seen as topics that any non-violent movement must
confront.

   The group also argues that there is a deep connection to the violence
of poverty and our culture's adherence to militarism; that both poverty
and militarism emerge from the same root, and that to resist one form of
violence requires resisting the other, interconnected, forms of oppression.
For instance, according to an early San Francisco Food Not Bombs flier
(figure 2.3):

> FOOD is a RIGHT not a *privilege*! Because there is enough food for
> everyone to eat! Because SCARCITY is a patriarchal LIE! Because a

The world produces enough food to feed everyone, if distributed equally. In fact, 46 billion pounds of food are discarded in this country each year. Estimates indicate that only 4 billion pounds of food would be required to end hunger in America. Food Not Bombs collects this surplus food before it reaches the dumpsters and distributes it directly to the hungry, outdoors in a public, non-institutional setting.

Because... FOOD is a RIGHT not a privilege / Because there is enough food for everyone to eat ! Because SCARCITY is a patriarchal LIE! Because a woman should not have to use her body to get a meal, or to have a place to sleep! Because when we are hungry or homeless we have the RIGHT to get what we need by panning, busking or squatting! Because POVERTY is a form of VIOLENCE NOT necessary or natural! Because capitalism makes food a source of profit not a source of nutrition! Because Food Grows On Trees. Because we need COMMUNITY NOT CONTROL! Because we need HOMES NOT JAILS! Because we need...

Food Not Bombs

1998 Food Not Bombs Calendar
IMPORTANT FACTS & DATES IN THE PEOPLE'S RESISTANCE TO REPRESSION · PHOTOS · QUOTES · ART

A FOOD NOT BOMBS MENU · 3145 GEARY BLVD. #12 · SAN FRANCISCO, CA 94118 · 1-800-884-1136

2.3 Food Not Bombs flier, 1998

woman should not have to USE HER BODY to get a meal, or have a place to sleep! Because when we are hungry or homeless we have the RIGHT to get what we need by panning, busking or squatting! Because POVERTY is a form of VIOLENCE not necessary or natural! Because capitalism makes food a source of profit not a source of nutrition! BECAUSE FOOD GROWS ON TREES. Because we need COMMUNITY CONTROL! Because we need HOMES NOT JAILS! Because we need . . . FOOD NOT BOMBS.

Within these statements, Food Not Bombs articulates an analysis of power relations that connect hunger, war, patriarchy, capitalism, homelessness, and violence to the same source. For many in Food Not Bombs it is the state and capitalism that have commodified food, objectified women, and punished the poor.

Our current food and economic system does not just perpetuate violence against humans; the commodification of food causes enormous violence to non-human animals and the natural world. As David Nibert (2002) persuasively shows, our current economic and social system has institutionalized violence against non-humans and, following the logic of violence that occurs with all oppressive relationships, naturalizes and justifies this repression. To Nibert and others within the animal rights community, non-humans experience extreme violence in nearly all aspects of their lives—from the forcible separation of children and mothers to the barbaric and horrific treatment they receive during their lives, to their eventual slaughter. Food Not Bombs, by serving only vegan and vegetarian food is taking a strong stance against the violence needed to ensure that meat, dairy, and eggs arrive on our plates.

The forms of violence opposed by Food Not Bombs, which are perpetuated by the capitalist economic system and the militaristic American state, are examples of a culture of death. According to this concept, our culture is constructed in such a way that large corporations exploit people, animals, and the earth. Our culture is a monstrous chimera of Gilgamesh and the blob: chopping down the cedars of Lebanon for the greatness of the nation and cannibalizing people and land for the sake of growth. This culture of death is predicated on viewing everything in the world as expendable and instrumental; there is no compassion, only an economic calculation to maximize.

Overall, this culture of death is not just oppressive and violent but also sick. In a culture of death, that which is destructive is seen as culturally valuable, and that which is constructive and loving is construed as abnormal. As Keith McHenry wrote:

> More than ever before, this death culture is pushing the idea that it is necessary for young people to join the army and kill to have peace. We have a society that suggests we can shop our way to a sustainable environment and poison our bodies to health. Peace through the threat of war is impossible because using the threat of destruction as a way to prevent war is nothing but domination. (McHenry, 2012: 19)

By engaging in the Orwellian practice of inverting good and bad, violence and peace, sick and healthy, the culture of death creates a destructive spiral. This spiral of violence and death, in being naturalized, means that empathy and love are tossed aside for the accumulation of wealth and alienation. The revolution that Food Not Bombs wants is against this culture of death. They wish to turn the world right side up before the culture of death turns into a collective suicide pact.

In contrast to this culture of death, Food Not Bombs calls for a culture of life, which requires that we rebuild our social and political institutions towards promoting and supporting life, love, and compassion. This means, according to McHenry, that:

> We want to replace this consumerist death culture with cooperative culture of "Daycare Not Warfare," "Clean Water Not Chemical Weapons,"

Vision Statement of San Francisco Food Not Bombs

Food not Bombs is a grassroots organization striving to work together cooperatively within our communities to build an egalitarian society. We are committed to a path of non-violence, within ourselves and for our world, compelling us to confront the many faces of violence including war, poverty, the prison and meat industries, environmental poisoning and destruction, imperialism, colonialism, police brutality, racism, cultural genocide, the objectification and degradation of women, and all forms of oppression including that based on race, class, gender, sexual orientation, lifestyle, ability or age.

Food not Bombs actively works for peace and justice grounded in consensus decision-making, collective action, feminism, equality, respect and honor for all life, the free flow of information; nurturance of body, mind, and soul...individual and community empowerment. We support affirmative action, police accountability, community conflict resolution, animal rights, reproductive choice and freedom, respectful child care, sustainable land use, responsible technologies, renewable energy, resource conservation and recycling , an economy based on cooperation and mutual sharing, and the basic human rights of food, homes, safety, dignity, education, genuine health care, meaningful and autonomous work and free and creative expression. Therefore we support radical democracy and we believe in Anarchism, with all the freedom and responsibility which are essential to this path.

Food not Bombs sponsors free community meals in public venues on a daily basis and at special events, demonstrations, and festivals. Our community meals aim at reclaiming public spaces from state and corporate control and ensuring that these places are open and safe for community use. In addition to vegetarian nourishment we offer informative literature and work in solidarity with other groups dedicated to radical change, locally and internationally. We actively support and participate in micro-powered free radio and socially conscious video, music, literature and art projects.

Food not Bombs utilizes surplus inherent in the prevailing food system and supports local organic distributors, farmers and community gardeners, which some of us are. We compost. Much of our work is accomplished using bicycles and bike trailers. The particular forms our work takes reflect the current situations and possibilities. Food not Bombs is part of the revolutionary movement which is everywhere creating the ideology and infrastructure of a new society.

We invite you to work with us to provide desperately needed services and information to our community. You can make a difference.

We meet every Thursday night @ the Epicenter Zone • 475 Valencia Street near 16th Street @ 7:30 PM

San Francisco FOOD NOT BOMBS • PO BOX 40485 • SANFRANCISCO, CA 94140 • 415 - 985 -7087

2.4 SF Food Not Bombs Vision Statement

"Food Not Lawns," "Homes Not Jails," "Really, Really, Really Free Markets," "Bikes not Bombs" and "Health Care Not Warfare." (McHenry, 2012: 19)

What we see here is a collection of life not death statements, that help highlight the different and complex ways that our current culture promotes violence on this world. In understanding violence as something so complex and multifaceted, the politics of Food Not Bombs presses all those committed to non-violence and social justice to become political outlaws and to fight against most facets of our society. For those who care about life, you cannot turn a blind eye to homelessness, to animal suffering, to mass incarceration, to rape culture, to the deportation of undocumented workers, to militarism, or to any other aspect of our culture that fetishizes death, suffering, and domination. To have empathy requires one to be a revolutionary.

This said, while Food Not Bombs provides a strong example of the anarchist intersectional power politics which dominated radical politics of the 1990s, there is space for critical engagement with their politics. For one, the politics they engage with can be seen as leveling difference and creating a blanket understanding that all oppressions are linked, and therefore operate similarly. But this is of course, not the case, as forms of structural oppression merge from different historical and political and economic realities and they serve different functions within the structure of modern American capitalism. For instance, while both patriarchy and white supremacy are essential aspects of American politics, it would be wrong to assume that race and gender operate the same as each other, and that we resist the two forms of oppression using similar strategies and tactics. The analysis that Food Not Bombs creates seems to reinforce the idea of oppression as a web. This claim is not necessarily wrong, but it makes more sense to think of oppression interlocking like a knotted ball of yarn; the different strands link together but often knot up, and sometimes pulling one string will actually reinforce and tighten the knot. A more complicated analysis of oppression opens up a theoretical space for understanding how struggles over homelessness and public space can, at times, conflict with other oppressed groups' interests. For instance, are there tensions between the homeless and working class or immigrant residents of the city? The criminologist Alex Vitale asserts that by not understanding the way that systems of oppression link homeless rights activists in New York pushed some working-class residents into the political hands of the neoconservative Giuliani (Vitale, 2009). For this reason any movement trying to radically transform society needs to understand the ways that class, race, and gender politics intersect. There is a possibility that the politics at the core of Food Not Bombs does not allow the space to do this and therefore limits the effectiveness of the group to build real and radical linkages between resistance to homelessness, white supremacy, speciesism, and the other systems of oppression they wish to confront.

Solidarity not charity

'Solidarity not charity' became a rallying cry for many of the grassroots activists involved with Common Ground in New Orleans. In calling for this change, the activists were calling for the non-governmental organizations, churches, and government relief agencies that descended on the city following the hurricane to reject the charity model and embrace a grassroots politics of mutual aid. In an UTNE reader article discussing this process, Sara Falconer wrote that:

> Real change in New Orleans—the kind that will give Norman's community a reason to return—will require solidarity of a different kind. It's not the "thousand points of light" feel-good charity work that George H. W. Bush championed. It's the rebirth of a civil rights-era approach that will put thousands of activists in direct confrontation with the state. (Falconer, 2010)

In critiquing the idea of charity, the activists from Common Ground, Food Not Bombs, and other radical social justice groups are tying charity to what the members of INCITE! Women of color have called the non-profit industrial complex.

According to Dylan Rodriguez, "the non profit industrial complex is a set of symbiotic relationships that link political and financial technologies of the state and owning class control with surveillance over public political ideology, including an especially emergent progressive and leftist social movements" (INCITE!, 2007: 8). The non-profit–industrial complex developed during the 1970s and 1980s and is marked by the professionalization of charity (turning charity into an industry), the proliferation of legal rules associated with 501(c)3 non-profit status, and the increased reliance on corporate donors and capitalist foundations for economic resources (mostly the Sage and Ford Foundations) (INCITE!, 2007: 3–7). The result is that charitable organizations transform into tools of capitalist and state interests. According to Andrea Smith, controlled charities perform in the following ways:

- Monitor and control social movements.
- Manage and control dissent in order to make the world safe for capitalism.
- Redirect activist energies into career-based modes of organizing instead of mass-based organizing capable of actually transforming society.

- Allow corporations to mask their exploitative and colonial work practices through "philanthropic" work.
- Encourage social movements to model themselves after capitalist structures rather than to challenge them. (Smith, 2007: 3)

While the rest of these aspects are all centrally important, for now I want focus on what Washawsky called non-profit quietism, which occurs when non-profits intentionally keep quiet on political and social issues out of fear of losing government or corporate contracts, or harming their 501(c)3 status.

This is an important aspect of homeless and hunger charity politics. According to Washawsky:

> food bank administrators have become cautious; the implication of disruption in government contracts are too serious to risk rocking the boat. Moreover, even though advocacy is legal for non-profits, the culture of fear created by government lobbying restrictions has prompted food bank administrators to dissuade employees from explicitly supporting particular positions on hunger, and institutional advocacy campaigns around the problems of hunger are increasingly rare. (Warshawsky, 2010: 771)

Thus neoliberal developments have declawed non-profits, limiting the ways in which they can advocate for social change. This allows the state to use the limited financial support, as well as tax and legal protections of non-profit status against critical and vocal non-profits and force them to act as stooges for status quo state interests.

While many non-profit and charity organizations have been co-opted by neoliberalism, some actively promote and encourage the perspective. Hackworth (J. Hackworth, 2010) examines religious charity groups and correctly concludes that these religious organizations tend to embrace neoliberal assumptions and actively encourage and promote neoliberalism to their supporters (church members) and to their clients (the homeless). Hackworth states: "the basic argument is that rescue missions offer a form of service that emphasizes individual and spiritual failures as the primary cause of one's plight" (J. Hackworth, 2010: 753). Most importantly, the churches see poverty and homelessness as the result of individual failings, rather than structural impediments, and see spreading the gospel as a means of helping the homeless find God and therefore get out of poverty. Therefore the vast majority of Christian rescue missions require people to attend church service in order to get access to meals or emergency beds. By conditioning meal and social service provisions on attending a religious mass, the churches are able to spread their message—mostly that homelessness is the direct result of not having faith—and support their message by almost always offering bible classes, while not always offering work training programs.[2] The individualized account of homelessness dovetails kindly with the neoliberal assertion that poverty is the result of bad decisions or character flaws (laziness, alcoholism, drug addiction, etc).

Finally, Poppendieck (1999) contends that neoliberal charity shifts the debate around social services from rights to gifts. Because demanding a better gift is disrespectful, the homeless are only entitled to what is gifted to them; this is not the case with a right. Every person can, and should, demand full access to what they are rightly entitled. In effect, neoliberalism depoliticizes food and affordable housing. This undermines advances made by the welfare rights movement, the homeless movement, and many other social justice movements.

In addition, Poppendieck claims that charity obfuscates the degree to which the state has defunded welfare provisions. Thus charity has allowed the state to cut its social service requirement, while not having nearly as much of an immediate shock to the poor and needy, who are able to get some services met through private non-profits. Poppendieck worries that over time, as the state decreases funds for poverty-related services, these benefits will be further diminished. In the meantime, non-profit charities provide a release valve for poor and marginalized members of society. The result is that non-profits mask some of the worst aspects of capitalism, from wealth inequality to political disempowerment. According to Poppendieck, charity diffuses some of the hostility and social pressure that would otherwise be directed in protest for social change.

Overall, the neoliberalization of the welfare state has drastically reduced social services, localized the distribution and funding of poverty programs, promoted an individualized rather than structural account of poverty and homelessness, and has looked to the market to further professionalize the industry. Overall this has limited the services available, made it so non-profits are less likely to engage in advocacy and activism, and disciplined the poor and homeless.

Food Not Bombs questions the politics of charity, non-profit quietism, and the non-profit industrial complex. This is not universally the case, however. Since Food Not Bombs is a radically decentralized movement, different chapters operate differently and many chapters actually fall back into the logic and process of charity politics, while others do not. Overall though, the logic of the movement and the official politics that have come out of McHenry and other important figures in the movement, seems to promote a politics in opposition to charity. This argument is put forward by Heynen (2010), where he highlights the hostile role Food Not Bombs has towards the concept of charity. He writes:

Unlike most charity, FNB works hard not to be complicit in the perpetuation of the capitalist states' biopolitics, but seeks to radically transform

> it. Unlike much charity, and because it is a movement of resistance, rather than amelioration, FNB might just threaten the developing, privatized modes of regulating the poor. FNB does this—in, however, a minor way—by cooking up not charity but mutual aid. (Heynen, 2010: 1233)

Thus, to Heynen, Food Not Bombs differs from charity because the group rejects biopolitics and radically attempts to alter the structures of society, not reinforce them. This concept of mutual aid instead of charity came up many times during interviews with former San Francisco Food Not Bombs members. Food Not Bombs embraces the logic of mutual aid by providing free food and solidarity with the homeless, hungry, and poor.

From the very beginning of the San Francisco chapter of Food Not Bombs, the organization intentionally tried to act differently from the charity organizations in the city. In interviews with former San Francisco Food Not Bombs members the majority of interviewees have highlighted the fact that the group intentionally decided to reject existing neoliberal conceptions of charity. For example, in an interview with an activist named "Steven," he claimed that the group's rejection of charity for a politics of solidarity was one of the most important aspects of the group. He contended that Food Not Bombs was not a charity group, and was actually hostile and opposed to the idea of charity. According to Steven, the group rejected charity by rejecting hierarchy in all its forms: there was no distinction between activists with Food Not Bombs and the hungry who came for the meal, and a large percentage of the group was comprised of homeless and formerly homeless activists. The group used consensus decision-making (the process championed by the Quakers that willingly engages in the time-consuming process of producing unanimity) and always engaged in solidarity with the homeless of the city. Steven saw the food distribution aspect of Food Not Bombs as a means of resisting the hierarchical and dehumanizing form of relations that is common at soup kitchens and government agencies. From this perspective, charity can be seen as depersonalized and cold. The humanizing and personalizing politics of Food Not Bombs put the group in stark contrast to government and religious charity models of food relief. The politics, organizational structure, and group membership of Food Not Bombs in San Francisco made food relief an act of solidarity and not an act of charity, law, or coercion.

Another way of resisting the concept of charity was the group's refusal (after 1991) to either ask the city for permits or to seek recognition as an official non-profit. In an interview with an early San Francisco Food Not Bombs activist "Kara," she mentioned that the group regularly debated both issues and every time came to the same conclusion: if they chose to pursue either permits or non-profit status they would become intertwined with the state, which would limit their power to resist, and if they were not able to politically resist, they would be failing in their commitment to be in solidarity with the poor and homeless of the city.

The massive week-long protest Food Not Bombs organized around the 50th anniversary of the UN is an ideal example of how the group combined mutual aid, solidarity, and oppositional politics. During this week-long event, which started on June 25, 1995, the group orchestrated a public occupation of UN Plaza, coordinated daily protests, and organized a 24-hour soup kitchen on the spot. While hundreds of groups protested the UN celebration—with topics ranging from AIDS to Tibet, the San Francisco police stated: "The one group that has been causing the most trouble this weekend is Food Not Bombs and, in my opinion, they would be the likeliest source of a problem" (Delgado, Winokur, & Allison, 1995).

In anticipation of the protest, Food Not Bombs put out a call to action, and turned the protest into a national Food Not Bombs gathering. Activists from nearly 40 chapters of Food Not Bombs—from Seattle to Boston—came to provide support. These reinforcements to the already large activist-base of Food Not Bombs allowed the group to maintain the soup kitchen and tent-city even with daily arrests and confiscations. In the first two nights alone, 73 Food Not Bombs activists were arrested for blocking intersections while an additional 9 were arrested for distributing food without a permit. Overall, the police and Food Not Bombs played a week-long cat-and-mouse game in which "day after day, in violation of city health ordinances, the activists smuggled bagels, soup and fruit into the plaza to feed the city's homeless. And day after day, the cops tried to prevent the food distribution, arresting numerous people in the process" (Delgado, Winokur, & Allison, 1995). By the end of the weekend-long action, the police appeared frustrated with arresting Food Not Bombs activists. Police Sergeant Rene Laprevotte told the *San Francisco Chronicle*, "We've been about 75 percent successful in intercepting the food before it's distributed. But to me it's just not worth the hassle. If they just let [Food Not Bombs] distribute their stuff, nine out of ten people wouldn't eat it. It's really crummy food." This massive protest is only one example of hundreds that highlight the ways that San Francisco Food Not Bombs combined its food distribution with political solidarity and confrontational politics. This event helped repoliticize homelessness in San Francisco and empower the homeless community to demand the end of hostile city policies.

The relationship that Food Not Bombs had with the logic of neoliberal charity poisoned their relationship with local charity groups. Because of this, the group had a hostile relationship with the vast majority of homeless charity groups in the city, with the exception of the more radical organizations like the San Francisco Coalition for the Homeless, the San Francisco Tenants Union, and the San Francisco chapter of the Catholic Workers.[3] Describing the debate over Food Not Bombs in a 1988 *San Francisco Chronicle* article, members of the homeless charity community—from the Salvation Army to the Catholic Missions—came out against the group (B. Gordon, 1988a). They felt that the group's politicization of food put homeless services at risk, and showed how the group was merely using the homeless to make an anarchist statement, a belief that was regularly cited by mayors Art Agnos and Frank Jordan.[4] In effect, Art Agnos, Frank Jordan, the charity industry, and the San Francisco police saw Food Not Bombs as using the homeless as a prop, while in reality the homeless were active political participants in Food Not Bombs.

What does it mean then to reject the neoliberal politics of charity? If the actions of Food Not Bombs are representative of such resistance, it means rejecting the professionalism and donation-centered politics of the non-profit industry. By rejecting these institutional pathways, it allows for Food Not Bombs to have a more confrontational politics and a more egalitarian and democratic organizational structure. It allows for a more confrontational politics since the support of social and economic elites or politicians is not needed for funding. In addition, if the group were tied to non-profit status, their confrontational and openly political stance would threaten their ability to keep this status. Embracing a charity model would force them to choose between their political agenda and the necessity of maintaining their non-profit status. Instead of worrying about these issues, Food Not Bombs is able to engage in a politics of solidarity, one that moves away from individual donation support, charitable volunteerism, and political lobbying, and towards a collectively oriented campaign against city policies that harm the hungry and homeless; in doing so, the group blurs the line between social service provider and radical political movement. This confrontational politics, however, is sometimes at odds with the group's interest in providing mutual aid. There is often a tension within local chapters between political conflict and providing as much food as possible to the hungry; at some points these two goals are mutually exclusive.

Build a new world in the shell of the old

Uri Gordon (U. Gordon, 2008) claims that one of the central tenets of contemporary anarchism is the idea of prefigurative politics, which is the attempt to live out political ideals through one's actions. Roughly, it means that activists must fuse their means with their ends. To promote a prefigurative politics requires peace activists to behave non-violently, for feminists to organize according to feminist principles, and for anti-capitalists to do what they can to reject the commodification of everyday life—possibly by promoting free economies and engaging in gift economies instead of monetary exchange. In short, to paraphrase the International Workers of the World slogan, prefigurative politics attempts to create a new world in the shell of the old, and its practitioners are not acting to create a revolution but living as if the revolution is happening.

Prefigurative politics was seen at the anti-globalization protests in Seattle "when protesters chanted 'this is what democracy looks like'." David

Graeber reminds us "they meant to be taken literally. In the best tradition of direct action, they not only confronted a certain form of power, exposing its mechanisms and attempting literally to stop it in its tracks: they did it in a way which demonstrated why the kind of social relations on which it is based were unnecessary" (Graeber, 2009: 84). According to Richard Day, a prefigurative politics also resides within "RTS [reclaim the streets], IMC [independent media collective], neighbourhood assembly, Social Centre, Food Not Bombs, land and factory occupation—all of these tactics consciously defy the logic of reform/revolution by refusing to work through the state, party, or corporate forms" (Day, R. J. F., 2005: 44–45). These organizations and tactics not only create temporary autonomous spaces but also because they prefigure the world the activists want to form, they also serve as a form of propaganda by the deed.[5] In fact, they serve as "the most effective form of anarchist propaganda" (U. Gordon, 2008).

In addition to just prefiguring their politics, groups like Food Not Bombs are also attempting to create alternative, dual power institutions to undermine the power of capitalism and the state. Originally, the concept of dual power emerged from Lenin's analysis of the February Revolution (Russia, 1917). In this period, the Bolshevik and provisional governments existed, claimed legitimacy and authority, and provided needed government services. In Lenin's understanding of the term, the alternative Bolshevik counterinstitution was a breeding ground for socialists to organize and successfully hollow out existing state institutions, allowing the revolution to succeed. According to Christopher Day from the North American Anarchist Federation, Love and Rage:

> in the broadest sense of the term, dual power refers to a situation in which a) parallel structures of governance have been created that exist side-by-side with old official state structures and that b) these alternative structures compete with the state structures for power and for the allegiance of the people and that c) the old state is unable to crush these alternative structures, at least for a period of time. (C. Day, 2003)

The strategy of dual power is attractive to anarchists, encouraging them to form alternative anti-capitalist institutions rooted in a radical form of democratic participation, and to challenge the dominant liberal and capitalist states. Anarchist Brian Dominick, in his article "An Introduction to Dual Power Strategy," lays out the anarchist application of dual power. He contends that:

> The dual power consists of alternative institutions which provide for the needs of the community, both material and social, including food, clothing, housing, health care, communication, energy, transportation,

educational opportunities and political organization. The dual power is necessarily autonomous from, and competitive with, the dominant system, seeking to encroach upon the latter's domain, and, eventually, to replace it. (Dominick, 2002)

In this regard, he follows the views of 1920s German anarchist Gustav Landauer, who in "For Socialism," argued that the state is not a material object but an expression of human relationships. These relationships cement themselves as institutions and, instead of trying to smash the state, which was the goal and desire of Bakunin and other nineteenth-century anarchists, radials should work to forge alternative institutions. These institutions needed to reflect the beliefs, desires, and goals of freedom, liberty, egalitarianism, and democracy (Landauer & Kuhn, 2010). It would be a mistake to view Landauer's statement against smashing the state as tantamount to turning alternative and counter institutions into passive vehicles that promote radical pluralism and democracy, but only in the fringes and cracks of society. Instead, it is important to note that dual power prefigurative institutions come into conflict with the state. This occurs whenever these institutions threaten the effectiveness and legitimacy of the state institutions— as chapter 3's discussion of autonomous versus state-oriented space will make clear. In effect, dual power acts as the constructive side of the direct action coin, serving as important spaces for direct democracy to play out and provide the material foundations for anarchist groups like Food Not Bombs to organize, build, and empower community.

This politics of alternative institutions and social relations is central to how most Food Not Bombs activists understand their public meals. In the 1992 *Food Not Bombs* book, Butler and McHenry express Food Not Bombs' prefigurative vision in this way:

> Food Not Bombs is an organization devoted to developing positive personal, political, and economic alternatives. Revolutionaries are often depicted as working to overthrow the government by any means necessary. Food Not Bombs groups in general do not have the time or resources to attack, tear down, and overthrow existing death culture. However, not spending our time trying to overthrow the existing power structure does not mean never struggling with it. By simply exerting our basic right to free speech and association, we challenge the power elite, and they will try to stop us from focusing on what needs to be done. We want to create new alternatives and life-affirming structures from the ground up. (Butler & McHenry, 2000: 72)

By engaging in direct action, Food Not Bombs finds solutions to hunger, homelessness and poverty by providing free meals, politically empowering the community, and by fighting alongside the homeless and petitioning the state to increase the number of homeless shelters and state-funded food banks. In creating the institutions needed to address the problems of hunger and homelessness themselves, Food Not Bombs is developing egalitarian, consensus-based duel power institutions. In creating these institutions, they provide space in which to address pressing social problems while empowering marginalized groups.

Conclusion

Howard Zinn's claim that Food Not Bombs' "slogan requires no complicated analysis" does not adequately describe the complexity of the group's politics: while they are committed to non-violence and addressing hunger and poverty, it is also about much more than that (Zinn, 2000). The group's understanding of violence as structural allows them to move beyond a single-issue critique of war, police violence, or homelessness, and instead to understand the interconnected nature of these forms of violence. In addition, by understanding violence as structural, Food Not Bombs seeks not just to address personal behavior, but to also to construct life-affirming social institutions.

To address the violence of our current culture, Food Not Bombs is actively trying to create an alternative, life-affirming, and democratic social institution. In embracing the anarchist conception of prefigurative politics, Food Not Bombs is not waiting for radical changes to capitalism and the state; nor is it petitioning and lobbying elected officials and government bureaucrats to do more. Instead they are building the new world in the shell of the old. In providing free meals in public space, Food Not Bombs creates alternative forms of political space while confronting state and corporate power. Finally, in rejecting the logic of charity, the group is not falling into the disempowering trap that many social service groups do.

This discussion of Food Not Bombs' political project is meant to provide the necessary background to see how the politics looks on the ground. The next few chapters will provide detailed discussion of how this radical project for a new world, centered on life and respect, clashes with the state and representatives of the "culture of death." The next chapter looks at what happens when San Francisco Food Not Bombs occupied public parks, turning them into a liberated space. In turning public parks into soup kitchens, radical meeting halls, tent-cities, and democratic symbols, the group came into conflict with the city of San Francisco, who viewed the parks as consumer spaces, not political spaces.

Notes

1 For this event, Food Not Bombs got hundreds of people to pee into drug-testing containers and mail them to the White House.

2 Work training programs, it is important to note, are also a form of neoliberal governmentality. In general, most "job training" programs start from the assumption that the reason someone is homeless or poor is because they do not have marketable skills. This assumes, much like all neoliberal poverty politics, that it is the person's own fault they are poor or homeless and does not question capitalism or any structural causes for poverty.

3 The situation in Orlando is very similar. There have been few charitable organizations that have openly supported Food Not Bombs, even though the new law negatively impacts the meal programs of many local churches; the only service-based organization that supports the group is the Vagabond Church, a church made up of homeless members, which does not have non-profit status and is as much a charitable pariah as is Food Not Bombs.

4 At one point Mayor Art Agnos attempted to force Food Not Bombs to serve at a local Unitarian food kitchen, even though the Unitarian charity had publicly come out against the direct action tactics of Food Not Bombs.

5 Commonly, propaganda by the deed is associated with acts of violence. This is generally the result of Bakunin and Sorel's influence within anarchist history but is not categorically the case. In general, propaganda by the deed refers to any action that is meant to inspire others to act in a similar way. As an example, consensus decision-making can serve as an example for other groups to follow, and therefore the deed or action itself serves as the form of propaganda.

3

Parks, permits, and riot police: understanding the politics of public space occupations 1988–1991

On a late afternoon in October of 2009, in San Francisco's United Nations Plaza, street vendors begin closing their shopping carts, packing their goods, and getting ready to go home. The plaza is filled with trucks, boxes, tables, and about thirty homeless people who are either sleeping on the grass or arguing on concrete makeshift benches. In the background, the gold dome of City Hall stands in stark contrast to those lying on the wet grass. Around nightfall, four people show up on bikes, carting plastic buckets of soup and a large black plastic bag filled with two-day old bread and bagels. Even with the street vendors clogging much of the square, a queue forms of homeless folks, traveler punks, and local activists. John, an off-again-on-again homeless man, hands out small fliers about the organization Food Not Bombs, while on the concrete slab, near the spot where the group has set up their soup, salad, and utensils, lies a pile of activist zines and fliers. Today's food serving, much like every serving since 1999, goes on without police conflict.[1] The closest the group comes to a police interaction is when a "sergeant" with the local Salvation Army, dressed in military-style attire, asks the food servers what church they are with. He walks away dumbfounded when the servers express that they are not with any church but are serving food as a protest to militarism, gentrification, and the city's hostility toward the homeless.

From 1988 to 1995, Food Not Bombs' food servings were not nearly as quiet. During that period, over a thousand Food Not Bombs activists were arrested or cited for distributing food without a permit, violating a court injunction, or resisting arrest. The response from the city was a mixture of humorous and horrific: they removed the benches that used to adorn UN Park, forcing all park residents to sit on wet grass and concrete ledges, they added threatening signs declaring that providing food without a permit is a misdemeanor, and the city spent taxpayers' dollars to remove a fountain from the Civic Center. Of course, the homeless are not there because of benches, soup, or views of beautiful fountains; they are there because capitalism creates extreme poverty.

This chapter is centered around 12 semi-structured formal and informal interviews I conducted with Food Not Bombs activists and local members of San Francisco's homeless activist community, over two 3-week periods in April 2010 and June 2011, as well as archival work done with the Art Agnos paper archives at the San Francisco Public Library and other newspapers, journals, and activist magazines. In this chapter I explore how the Agnos administration used permits as a means of forcing Food Not Bombs into what criminologists have called negotiated management, a policing procedure that creates formal and informal ties between police and protest groups. Negotiated management was meant to include the group within the institutional structures of the state-charity nexus, and thereby moderate the group's activism and regulate their political practices in public spaces. The primary reason for the conflict between the progressive Art Agnos and Food Not Bombs is due to tensions that arose when the democratic and autonomous politics of Food Not Bombs clashed with the sovereign political claims of city officials. As such, this case highlights the way that different conceptions of space—sovereigntist, representational populist, and autonomous populist—can come into conflict and open up new political opportunities to make marginalized voices audible, hidden bodies visible, and state coercive power apparent.

Public space, negotiation, and the politics of occupation

The democratic potential of public space makes it both a powerful force for emancipatory politics and a dangerous locus of disorder and violence. Expressing this, Benjamin Shepard and Greg Smithsimon look at Dolores Park in San Francisco and highlight the fact that "in this compressed, urban park only a couple of blocks long, there is a marvelous integration of different users of the space, but simultaneously firm self-segregation as well" (Shepard and Smithsimon, 2011: 5). What makes Dolores Park exciting and powerful to the authors is the fact that the control and regulation of the space "is not emanating from the squad car. Order in public space is generated primarily, though not exclusively in this case, by the users" (Shepard and Smithsimon, 2011: 5). While, of course, Dolores Park is regulated by the city of San Francisco and monitored by the San Francisco police, the authors are correct in asserting that the day-to-day politics of Dolores Park is regulated not by city code, but by the users of the park. Basketball players negotiate the space with families playing on swings, as well as with tourists taking vacation photos, and city residents relaxing on the grass having lunch. Why does the democratic nature of this space matter?

Democratic public space matters because public space is, historically, one of the few sites of political contestation for marginalized and excluded bodies. For instance, throughout US history, female, non-whites, queer, disabled, and lower-class bodies and voices have been excluded from public spaces and democratic involvement. Yet the inclusion of these bodies into the political community first occurred through the occupation and claiming of public space. The ability of these groups to make themselves politically visible was central to their inclusion. This is why Don Mitchell argued that we need to fight to preserve the openness and vibrancy of public space; occupying public space is one of the ways the marginalized can create "a place for representation" that allows their voices to be heard (Mitchell, 2003). This argument is repeated by other theorists, such as Benjamin Shepard, who has argued that it was largely through reclaiming public spaces that queer and non-white bodies have been able to incorporate themselves into the public sphere (Shephard and Smithsimon, 2011).

But the relationship between public space and citizen involvement is complex, especially for the homeless. This is because, as Leonard Feldman (2006) states, the homeless serve as one of the others that are used to define citizenship in a liberal democracy. To Feldman, liberal citizenship is directly connected with the public/private divide, and to be a full citizen in a liberal society, one is required to have a private space that they can return to. In other words, to Feldman, the political inclusion problem for the homeless has nothing to do with their invisibility but with their hyper-visibility, by the fact that they have no way of escaping the public eye (Feldman, 2006). This idea is reasserted by Tony Sparks (2012) who, in looking at homelessness policy in King County, Washington, notes how city officials discounted the voices and opinions of the homeless because they were, de facto, defined as being unable to manage their own lives and thus needed to have their lives managed for them. He writes:

Today's homeless are caught in a double-bind wherein they must choose between pathologization and criminalization as a condition of basic survival . . . While the latter aims at physical exclusion of bodies from public space, the former, in effect if not in intent, marks the exclusion of the homeless from full citizenship in the public sphere. (Sparks, 2012: 1518)

Simply by being homeless, one is considered to lack the rationality, reason, and self-regulation that is required for liberal democratic involvement. It seems what makes public space a potential location for political self-representation is not its visibility, since, as Feldman points out, that visibility is double-edged, but the potential for democratic engagement and participation that it allows.

Overall, public space becomes a location for political contestation and a site for political mobilization. The theorists, above all, state that the more democratic the space, the more likely it is for marginalized bodies to resist their exclusion and politically represent themselves. Of course, there are those who oppose democratic space, for just this reason. Those who value top-down order and the maintenance of the status quo view democratic public space as a threat. This is because, as Simon Springer asserts, "public space is understood as a battlefield on which conflicting interests of the rich and poor are set" and this conflict occurs because "the inherently contested nature of public space reveals that it is never free from the risk of disorder, an observation that places democracy in conflict with the need for 'order' so that the capital should flow smoothly" (Springer, 2011: 528). This struggle between democratic vibrancy and sovereign order is central to Margaret Kohn's typology of space into sovereign and populist space, but her conception of space does not understand the value of a third type of space— autonomous space. I argue that *autonomous populist space* offers a militant counter to non-autonomous populist space, what I call representative populist space.

The top-down perspective of public order is inherently consumerist. According to Don Mitchell, this approach is "one of open space for recreation and entertainment, subject to usage by an appropriate public that is

3.1 Riot police surrounding a Food Not Bombs table in the Haight District, Labor Day 1988

allowed in. Public space thus constituted a controlled and orderly retreat where a properly behaved public might experience the spectacle of the city" (Mitchell, 1995: 115). Margaret Kohn refers to this counter view of public space as sovereign space. This perspective accepts the Hobbesian conception of unitary sovereignty, and from there asserts, "Something is public if it is authorized by legitimate state institutions" (Kohn, 2013: 101). This means that, from the sovereign view, public space only exists as a construct of the state, and therefore the state has absolute sovereignty in regulating and managing it.

The sovereign view of public space has two features:

First, it takes for granted the separation between the rulers and the ruled. Even when Sovereignty is vested in representative assembly rather than a monarch, there is still a sense that public power is something distinct from the aggregate of citizen-subjects. The second feature is a consequence of the first. The state has a monopoly over legislating and enforcing the law and citizens have a responsibility to comply. (Kohn, 2013: 102)

In arguing for the state's monopoly over public space, combined with neo-liberal dictates in support of corporate economic power, the sovereign view tends to a conception of the ordered city that values space not in respect to its use-value, but instead its exchange-value (Lefebvre & Nicholson-Smith, 2011). In effect, the sovereign view in most US cities means that the state orders public space for the benefit of economic interests and not for public good or resident use. The contemporary sovereign view pushes the city to develop as a sanitized city, which is preferred by tourists, wealthy residents, and corporate interests. As the recent protests against Google buses in San Francisco show, there is a substantial resistance to this conception of the city, and to corporate controlled public space, so much so that a sovereign conception of space requires non democratic top-down regulation, the limiting of access, and the policing of dissent.

Margaret Kohn, Don Mitchell, and others have noted that the restrictive vision of sovereign space often provides an impetus for resistant movements. To such movements, reclaiming public space allows for the contesting of the political exclusions that plague the political system. When the order of sovereign space breaks down, what erupts is, according to Kohn, populist space.

Kohn "uses the term populist because it signals the political mobilization of the people outside the institutional structures of the state" (Kohn, 2013: 103). This conception of space is collectively constructed, and is extra-parliamentary. It is "because aggrieved citizens can express the intensity of their discontent through protest and non-compliance, [that] the government is forced to negotiate and compromise, thereby incorporating the people's desires into the law" (Kohn, 2013: 103). In effect, to Kohn, populist space exists whenever a power from below reclaims public space and turns that space into a form of what Don Mitchell calls representational space. This means that the defining feature of populist space is its ability to make visible the excluded views and perspectives of the populace. An example of populist space is described in Don Mitchel's (2003) work on the protests over Berkeley, California's People's Park. He asserts that the protests forced the University administrators and city officials to include the homeless in their political calculations and pressured the city to engage in negotiation with the activists in the park. Of course not all populist claims to space are the same, as there is a fundamental difference between anarchistic occupations of a park and permitted rallies on a street corner.

In not examining the tension between permitted and non-permitted public protests, theorists like Kohn and Mitchell miss the importance that autonomous claims have in providing the militant edge to populist space. Jenny Pickerill and Paul Chatterton define autonomous spaces as, "those spaces where people desire to constitute non-capitalist, egalitarian, and solidaristic forms of political, social, and economic organization through a combination of resistance and creation" (Pickerill & Chatterton, 2006: 1). This means that autonomous space is inherently anti-capitalist, radically democratic, and resistant.[2] The confrontational nature of autonomous space is what makes it different from traditional representational populist space, which is not inherently anti-capitalist or democratic, merely dissident. Autonomous populist space rejects the state's authority to monopolize control over public space and is thus a direct refusal of the logic inherent in the sovereign definition of space. Against the representational populist conception of space, this autonomous understanding is not primarily concerned with appealing to governing elites, but in generating non-hierarchical, non-capitalist, user-based democratic spaces that serve as a counter institution to the state. This is why Occupy Wall Street created peoples' assemblies, free schools, free libraries, free medical clinics, etc. Occupy Wall Street and anarchistic public space occupations are about experiments in direct democracy. Again, this does not mean that there are no political claims or demands being made during occupations, only that their goal *is not* to get a seat at the decision table, but instead to reject the idea that decisions should be made behind closed doors. Overall, then, autonomous claims should not be seen as separate from populist space—for when autonomous claims occur in public they are inherently representational as well as prefigurative—but instead as a subcategory of populist space. Thus, in adding to Kohn, I contend that we examine space as being sovereigntist, representational populist, and autonomous populist.

Creating this separation between representational and autonomous forms of populist space is important in developing a more complete understanding of how political resistance works. The majority of populist claims on space are, in fact, not autonomous from the state as they accept protest permits that tie them into the logic of sovereign space. In doing so, the goal of populist space becomes collapsed into merely being a space for representation; its political demand becomes, quite simply, political acceptance and inclusion. However, this view is problematic for protest movements, because negotiation and inclusion is often the desire of state agencies and police forces. This can be seen most clearly by usage of negotiated management by police forces in the United States and Europe. Negotiated management seeks to create ties between police and protest groups, commonly through a lengthy permitting process, in which representatives from the police and activists negotiate time, place, and restrictions for actions (McPhail, Schweingruber, & McCarthy, 1997). The police rely on direct communication with protestors as a means of collecting information about them, and use the negotiation to tailor protests (in terms of location, size, etc.) to better ensure social control and stability. For groups that negotiate with them, police commonly provide concessions; Luis Fernandez mentions, "When they properly apply the model, police offer movement leaders concessions in exchange for an agreement to self-police and to outline the scale, route, and timing of demonstrations" (Fernandez, 2008: 13). The goal, then, of negotiated management is to delimit the space for protestors to engage in symbolic political protest, which limits disruption to social, political, and economic sites. Thus negotiated management seeks to incorporate and institutionalize protestors as a means of pacifying and regulating them. In effect, negotiated management is a form of interaction between protestors and the state that does not question the unequal power relations between the two sides. When protestors negotiate on the state's terms, they are doing so in a very disadvantageous position, as they have no political leverage to pressure the state with. Instead of being fair and equal negotiations, in which the protest movement makes demands of the state, this situation is more commonly defined by protest movements conceding to the demands and interests of the state for fear of government repression. I argue that successful autonomous populist movements threaten the state and, therefore, when they negotiate or interact with the state, they do so from a better political position and are able to make strong political demands because of this position.

In the rest of this chapter, I look at how San Francisco Food Not Bombs, an autonomous political movement, conflicted with the Art Agnos administration in San Francisco. This narrative highlights three things: the role of permits and negotiated management by the city as an attempt to control and regulate public space; the power of autonomous movements to open up political space that would not otherwise be opened; and the political impact that contested space has on local urban politics.

Setting the scene: Agnos and the state of politics in San Francisco 1988–1991

Art Agnos, a former California Assembly member, entered the 1987 San Francisco mayoral campaign as the most progressive candidate in the race. He ran on his longstanding support of women's, labor, and environmental rights as a progressive CA Assembly member. During the 1987 campaign, urban political scientist Richard DeLeon claimed that Agnos appealed directly to the three segments of the political left in San Francisco: social liberals, environmentalists, and political populists (DeLeon, 1992: 91).

Agnos was elected mayor on his progressive credentials, but the realities of San Francisco municipal politics strained his progressive coalition. Under the previous mayor, Diane Feinstein, San Francisco had experienced ten years of pro-growth urban development, which had rendered San Francisco one of the most thoroughly gentrified cities in the country by the mid-1980s (Zukin, 1987). As an example of gentrification privileging, the requirements of the urban elite over the needs of low-income people, the number of single occupancy hotel rooms citywide was cut by nearly half from 1975 to 1988, while the number of upscale hotel rooms nearly doubled (Hartman, Carnochan, & Hartman, 2002: 368). Likewise, urban redevelopment at the Yerba Buena Center and in the Mission district expanded office space and new middle-class condos but destroyed over ten thousand low-income apartments and single occupancy rooms.[3] The low-income units were never rebuilt and the condos that replaced them are deeply implicated in the exponential rent increases in San Francisco. Feinstein's neoliberal policies not only shrunk the availability of low-income housing but also seriously stressed the city's coffers, leaving Agnos to inherit a budget shortfall of $172 million (Hartman, Carnochan, & Hartman, 2002: 256). Even though these problems were not his doing, Agnos was unable to deflect blame for the city's budget problems. *San Francisco Examiner* columnist Bill Mandel named Agnos "the Velcro Mayor" since everything stuck to him.

One of the Agnos administration's most ambitious programs dealt with the city's homeless, with his *Beyond Shelters* proposal. Agnos had campaigned to humanely address structural causes of homelessness by shifting away from the shelter system model towards developing low-income housing. The program would have also expanded the availability of job training, mental health services, and addiction recovery programs. But by the end of his term the only major development for the city's homeless was, ironically, the development of two new shelters. Agnos also spearheaded several punitive policing campaigns against the homeless. In 1988 he revived a 1972 city ordinance against car camping in an attempt to remove homeless people from the Haight district. He also revived a forgotten nineteenth-century city ordinance against "lodging" (known as section 647[i]), which made lying down with camping gear illegal. Under this ordinance, falling asleep under blankets or sleeping bags could result in citation and arrest for illegally "lodging" in public. Finally, towards the end of his term, Agnos began using the police to sweep city parks of the homeless (Hartman, Carnochan, & Hartman, 2002: 378).

Richard DeLeon has suggested that Agnos had neither the patience nor the power to enact his progressive agenda, pursuing instead "the path of least resistance" (DeLeon, 1992: 159). Instead of listening to and working with the city's grassroots sectors as promised, Agnos continued Feinstein's neoliberal development policies and gentrification projects. Presuming that urban development easily created jobs and increased revenue to the city, Agnos abandoned his platform of neighborhood and community diversity and respect, as well as his promises to reform the city's homelessness policies. This led to Agnos being viewed "as a bait-and-switch political con artist who got himself elected as a slow-growth progressive but then governed the city as a pro-growth liberal" (DeLeon, 1992: 158). Agnos saw his coalition fall apart as two former Allied council members ran against him in 1991, neither candidate endorsing him in his run-off election against conservative Democrat Frank Jordan. Progressives in San Francisco saw Jordan, the former police chief running as a pro-business, pro-development candidate, as no worse than their former golden boy Art Agnos.

From permits to "Camp Agnos": Food Not Bombs public occupations and the contested nature of homelessness politics in San Francisco

The San Francisco chapter of Food Not Bombs started in December 1987, when Keith McHenry, the co-founder of Food Not Bombs and a recent émigré to San Francisco from Boston, organized a Food Not Bombs meal near Golden Gate Park with the help of the Haight Ashbury Neighborhood Council. The meal consisted largely of rice, beans, and bread, served from plastic buckets into makeshift bowls and cups.

On July 11, 1988, the group placed itself on the city's radar by applying for a parks permit, so they could legally distribute the food in Golden Gate Park.[4] Around the same time, the Cole Valley Improvement Association, a group of business owners and developers in the Haight District, began pressuring the city to stop the group's activities. They argued that free public meals were attracting the wrong type of people to the neighborhood—the homeless, poor, and transient—which they claimed resulted in a profoundly negative impact on the quality of life within the Haight.[5]

FOOD NOT BOMBS
3145 Geary Boulevard, #12, San Francisco, CA 94118 (415) 885-6245, ext. 1

July 11, 1988

Mr. Peter Ashe
Mc Laren Lodge
Golden Gate Park
San Francisco, CA 94112

Dear Mr. Ashe,

We would be interested in a permit to provide free meals and information
at the corner of Haight and Stanyan Streets in the park.

Both Pablo Hasing and John Meehan have suggested we write you about this
matter.

We serve approximately 150 vegetarian meals, which are very nutritious.
Our labor and food is donated, and we only ask for donations at our
tables. We are filling a time slot not filled by any other local food
providers. At the present, that time is Mondays from 10 a.m. to 5 p.m.

Food Not Bombs has been serving meals to the needy since 1980, and has
a good record of maintaining a clean operation. We have support of the
community for this project, and know that you will find us very
welcome guests at the Golden Gate Park.

Sincerely,

Keith Mc Henry

001482

3.2 Picture of city permit 1988

Shortly after the Cole Valley Improvement Association complained, the city denied Food Not Bombs a park permit. Starting on August 15, 1988, and continuing on and off for the rest of the Agnos administration, police arrested members of the group en masse, confiscated their equipment and literature, and donated their food to local churches.[6] On the first day of arrests, the police sent fourteen officers to arrest nine people for "distributing food without a permit," which was an infraction, not a misdemeanor. When asked by a reporter for the *San Francisco Chronicle* about the Food Not Bombs arrests, police spokesman Jerry Senkir stated, "This appears to be more of a political statement than a program to feed the hungry. We cannot allow them to take over the park" (B. Gordon, 1988a: A3). The

Date	Permit issue
12/27/87	FNB starts feeding homeless in San Francisco parks
07/11/88	FNB requests a permit from the San Francisco Recreations and Parks Department
08/15/88	Forty-five riot police arrest nine volunteers for serving free food in Golden Gate Park
08/27/88	Twenty-nine people arrested for serving free food in Golden Gate Park
09/01/88	Fifty-two people arrested for serving free food in Golden Gate Park
09/09/88	Mayor Agnos issues the first permit (a sixty-day temporary permit) to FNB to serve free food in Golden Gate Park after two days of direct negotiations
02/01/89	San Francisco Recreation and Parks Department issues a second temporary permit for FNB feedings in Golden Gate Park
07/21/89	City files an injunction against serving free food without proper permits, during a homeless tent-city in Civic Center
09/11/89	The Health Department issues FNB its first health permit for feeding at Golden Gate Park
02/01/90	San Francisco Recreation and Parks Department, and Fire and Health Departments provide FNB a permit to serve food at the Civic Center
07/06/90	The San Francisco Recreation and Parks Department passes a law making it significantly more difficult for anyone to be issued a permit to distribute free food outdoors, FNB loses its parks permit
01/25/91	Keith McHenry (FNB co-founder) is served with contempt papers for breaking a court injunction prohibiting food distribution activities
02/14/91	The city asks that McHenry serve forty days in jail for violation of court order
03/22/91	Judges dismiss the injunction charges

Note: This table was generated by using information regarding permits from the Food Not Bombs Menu (their newsletter) and by including additional information gained through interviews and newspaper articles.

3.3 Chronology of permits issued to Food Not Bombs

political nature of the group was central to the city's response. This is clearly seen by internal mayoral documents found in the Agnos archives. In an August 29, 1988, report to the mayor, it was stated "Food Not Bombs are trying to manipulate the homeless situation for political purposes and should not be allowed to ignore permit requirements. It is OK for Mother Teresa to ignore same permits because she is pure of heart. This division of good guys and bad guys in terms makes enforcement selective" [*sic*] (anonymous, 1988).

Within a month, the antagonism between the city and the group came to a head when, on Labor Day 1988, two hundred hungry and homeless people went to Golden Gate Park in search of a hot meal while fifty-two activists from Food Not Bombs, surrounded by riot police, lined up to serve them food. The riot police counted twenty-five served meals, the legal number allowed by city law before breaking permit restrictions, and then began arresting people. The arrests proceeded like an assembly line: an activist would scoop a bowl of food and hand it to a hungry person and a police officer would then handcuff and arrest that activist. Echoing the spirit of the 1909 Wobblies' free-speech fights in Spokane, the next activist in line to serve would take up the ladle, serve another bowl of food and promptly be arrested by another police officer. This process continued until all fifty-two activists had been arrested. The arrests garnered national news attention from the *New York Times*, CNN, and other mainstream media outlets.

After the Labor Day arrests, on September 8, 1988, the city claimed it would cease arresting the activists in exchange for Food Not Bombs agreeing to negotiate the location of free meals with the city. According to Bob Prentice, then city coordinator for homeless programs, the mayor's office did not "want to be in a position of arresting people because they're giving good food to hungry people" (Gordon, 1988: A3). The city declared a ceasefire from arrests when members of Food Not Bombs, the ACLU, the Police Department, and the city sat down to negotiate a solution to the problem. Under the terms of the agreement, Food Not Bombs would move its meal distribution activities a few blocks away to the corner of Stanyan and Page (which was not in Golden Gate Park), and would secure permits from the San Francisco Recreation and Parks Department. In exchange, the city would provide a sixty-day temporary permit, waive the $400 fee, and drop all charges against Food Not Bombs activists. Agnos stated in the press conference, "in enforcing the law, we don't want to create a remedy that is [more] work than the problem" and that "we must develop a policy for this kind of program, where people can be fed with dignity and in privacy" (Halstuk, 1988: A3). Interestingly, Agnos seemed more concerned with the public aspect of the meals than with the health and safety issue, as noted in his insistence on privacy. This subtlety might explain why activist materials were confiscated and the food was donated to local churches. If the city was concerned about food safety in a public setting, why would they stipulate that unused food by Food Not Bombs be distributed through other charity groups in private?

Though Food Not Bombs secured a temporary sixty-day permit on September 9, 1988, the debate and politics surrounding a permanent permit continued (see figure 3.3). A few months after the first permit was issued, the San Francisco Recreation and Parks Department changed its laws regarding permitting. The public consultation to discuss the new permit requirements drew over 300 people, and the vast majority showed their support for Food Not Bombs. This turnout broke the attendance record for a Recreation and Parks Department meeting (Whitting, 1989: B3–4). The new permits law toughened the sanitation rules concerning tables, metal containers, and hand-washing stations. One of the reasons for the changing permit requirements might concern the fact that, according to the mayor's staff, "Rec-Park does not issue food distribution permits lightly because it does not want to encourage use of parks as homeless encampments" (Agnos archives). Despite the stricter rules, the city gave Food Not Bombs a permit

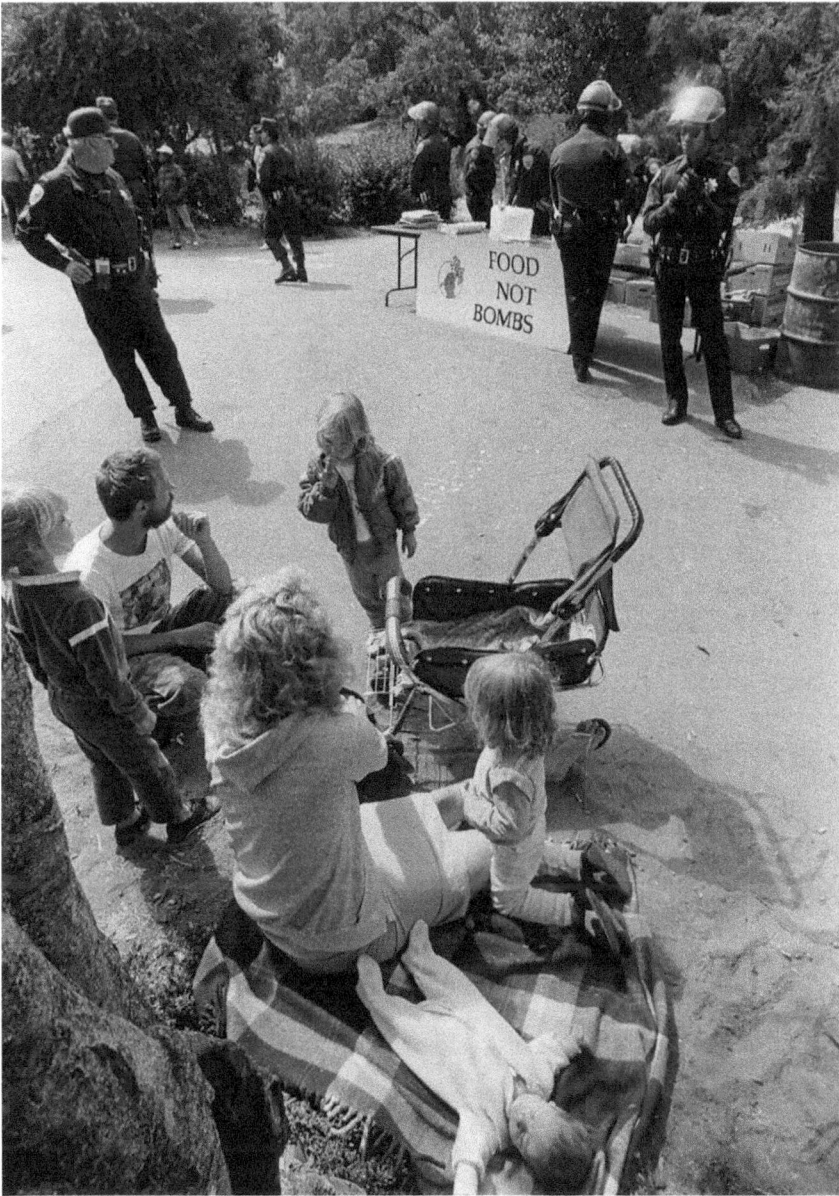

3.4 Children in front of Food Not Bombs arrest

PERMIT TO OPERATE
AND CERTIFICATE OF SANITARY INSPECTION

D 2260

Issued according to provisions of the San Francisco Health Code

AUTHORIZING conduct of the following class of premises

Non-Fee Permit

ISSUED

March 13, 1990

Food Not Bombs
DBA: FOOD NOT BOMBS
Civic Center
San Francisco, CA

THIS PERMIT TO OPERATE MAY BE REVOKED OR SUSPENDED FOR CAUSE AND IS NOT TRANSFERABLE. CHANGE OF OWNERSHIP must be reported immediately.

DEPARTMENT OF PUBLIC HEALTH
City and County of San Francisco

DEPARTMENT OF PUBLIC HEALTH — 101 GROVE STREET — SAN FRANCISCO, CALIFORNIA 94102

Display this Permit prominently. This margin may be trimmed for standard 6 x 8 frame.
H.C. #5

PERMIT TO OPERATE
AND CERTIFICATE OF SANITARY INSPECTION

D 2258

Issued according to provisions of the San Francisco Health Code

AUTHORIZING conduct of the following class of premises

TEMPORARY FOOD FACILITY (MONDAY ONLY)

ISSUED

September 11, 1989

Non-Fee Permit

Food Not Bombs
c/o Keith McHenry
DBA: FOOD NOT BOMBS
Page & Stanyan Streets
San Francisco, CA

THIS PERMIT TO OPERATE MAY BE REVOKED OR SUSPENDED FOR CAUSE AND IS NOT TRANSFERABLE. CHANGE OF OWNERSHIP must be reported immediately.

DEPARTMENT OF PUBLIC HEALTH
City and County of San Francisco

DEPARTMENT OF PUBLIC HEALTH — 101 GROVE STREET — SAN FRANCISCO, CALIFORNIA 94102

3.5 Food Not Bombs permits 1989 and 1990

to provide meals at the corner of Stanyan and Page (the negotiated location) on February 1, 1989—almost a year after negotiations began.

The permit was short lived. On June 28, 1989, Food Not Bombs organized a 24-hour soup kitchen for a tent-city protest in the Civic Center Park, right in front of City Hall. The three-week tent-city became known as Camp Agnos, and embraced the slogan "We're tired, we're hungry, we don't like the government" (Edmondson, 2000: 48). Homeless activists protested about the failure of the Agnos administration to address the issue of homelessness and affordable housing within the city. Unlike mainstream homeless organizations, Camp Agnos activists engaged in direct action, creating a public spectacle in front of City Hall.

Agnos attempted to ignore the mass of people sleeping in front of his workplace, but on July 11 his administration arranged a town hall meeting on homelessness and invited members from Camp Agnos to speak. At that meeting, thirteen homeless people addressed the mayor about the need for public bathrooms, storage lockers, public showers, affordable housing, medical centers, detoxification centers, and other government services. Although most of these demands were components of Agnos's promised *Beyond Shelters* plan, the Agnos administration openly opposed any concession to the protestors (with the exception of allowing people to cover themselves with blankets at night) because he feared that concessions could make the encampment more permanent.

Protesting about Agnos's failure to respond to the tent-city occupants at the town hall meeting, the next day Food Not Bombs members occupied the mayor's office and demanded immediate action to help the city's homeless. The office occupation angered the administration: afterwards, Agnos refused to meet with any representative from Camp Agnos and began arresting tent-city protestors generally, not just Food Not Bombs activists. By the end of the over three-week tent-city occupation, approximately twenty people had been arrested.

In the midst of the occupation, the mayor's office revoked Food Not Bombs' permit and filed a lawsuit against them. Assistant City Attorney George Riley explained, "All the City is attempting to do is enforce minimum safety standards ... We don't seek to enjoin any expressive activities" (Bodovitz & Miyasato, 1989: A3). The injunction served as a deterrent for some activists and provided an easy way for the police to remove the group from public space, confiscating their literature, tables, and pots, and generally increasing the cost of activism in order to persuade the group to accept forced inclusion and moderation of their politics. Increasing the costs of acting was actually one of the proposed ways of addressing the group, according to an internal mayoral administration memo. In this memo, the anonymous author stated that the city should "use fines in conjunction with citations to put financial pressure on McHenry and Food Not Bombs" and "use the homeless network to isolate Food Not Bombs by stressing that agitation is destructive to the entire food distribution network" (Agnos archive).

Though tickets and citations had a heavy cost for the activists, it was the permit process that was the central means through which mayor Agnos attempted to institutionalize and incorporate the group. The lack of a permit justified police harassment and allowed the state to force a negotiation between representatives of Food Not Bombs, the Police Department, and the mayor's office. The object of these negotiations was to get the group to accept a location shift away from tourist areas and gentrifying neighborhoods. Lieutenant Holder stated, "If they're truly concerned with feeding the people, there is a better place for it" (Gordon, 1988: A3). The "better place," according to the city, was in a church warehouse at Stanyan and Page. These better places were private while the more tourist and business-centered locations were defined as "out-of-place" (Wright, 1997). Of course, Food Not Bombs was always hostile to the idea of changing the location. When the idea of moving was first brought up, Keith McHenry stated: "We are going to continue doing this until we have ended hunger and poverty—that's going to take a while" (B. Gordon, 1988b: A5). Unwillingness to move and unwillingness to compromise the organization's position made for an obvious political tension. One of the group's main opponents, Therese Gaus from the Cole Valley Improvement Association, stated: "[the public meals] creates a situation that is likely to embarrass the Mayor" (Gordon, 1988: A5).

While the city used health and safety permits as a means of regulating public space, Food Not Bombs asserted that serving free food should not require a permit. According to McHenry, "Anybody who's got food should be able to feed anybody who's hungry" (Gordon, 1988: A3), and, "It's the same thing as regulating Christmas presents" (Whitting, 1989: B3–4). In addition, he mentioned during the tent-city protest, "This is people sharing free food with their friends. Under no circumstances would a health permit be necessary. We will never stop feeding people" (Johnson, 1989: A2). What Food Not Bombs' actions came to highlight was the way that permits were intentionally used by the city to regulate the homeless community.

The city saw Food Not Bombs as a threat to the maintenance of public order because activists refused to keep meals and direct action within acceptable spaces. In Bob Prentice's July 18 testimony before the board of supervisors, he highlighted that the mayor's goal with the tent-city was to "distinguish between the encampments of homeless people and Food Not Bombs." In doing so, he distinguished between good homeless groups that met with the mayor, and bad groups like Food Not Bombs, who seemed recalcitrant (Agnos archive). In making his argument against Food Not Bombs, Prentice provided an overview of the group's failed attempts at getting a health code permit, their hostility to the San Francisco Recreation and Parks Department service regulations, but never mentioned the arrests of activists, confiscation of property, or the fact that in every public meeting about the organization they seemed to have massive public support. In the end Prentice claimed "Food Not Bombs has an understandable agenda that goes beyond just serving food to homeless people. They raise questions about political priorities in the nation that many of us share. However, when their agenda interferes with even basic measures to assure the safety of the food they serve, they deserve neither sympathy nor the right to claim that their refusal advances the interests of homeless people" (Agnos archive). Paradoxically, the city's attempt to govern the actions of Food Not Bombs within the homeless encampment actually produced public disorder, since whenever police arrested people for distributing food, tensions would escalate, as homeless residents were angry and resisted having their meals stolen from them. With City Hall seeing the tent-city as "a very violent ugly incident" that had the potential to "make San Francisco look like Tiananmen Square," the city wanted to exclude the group most directly involved in refusing state control and the city's policing tactics (Bodovitz, 1989: A1).

Since Food Not Bombs, after their first attempt with the permitting process, was not willing to compromise, moderate their stance, or remove themselves from public view, the state used the police to harass the organization—arresting and citing the activists for a small infraction that countless other organizations and individuals break on a daily basis. This

3.6 Police confiscating milk crates from Civic Center

interaction highlights the way that permits are used to control and force radical movements into the regulatory confines of the state.[7]

Autonomous politics and the struggle over space and representation

The struggle between Food Not Bombs and the Agnos administration is about sovereign and autonomous populist claims to public space clashing. In this conflict, the city of San Francisco attempted to negotiate a solution that maintains their sovereign claims over public space. As such, the purely representational components of the public park occupations were accepted by the city, as they seemed interested in opening space for homeless voices to be included in the decision-making process. This is seen, not only by Agnos's willingness to negotiate and work with Food Not Bombs as long as they move from autonomous politics, but also by his willingness to negotiate and compromise with other homeless rights groups during the tent-city. In both these examples, the administration responded to the occupations by constructing a solution that expanded inclusion in exchange for groups giving up their more radical positions.

The narrative described in this chapter also highlights the confrontational nature of autonomous claims to space. The public meals and tent-cities organized by Food Not Bombs empowered subaltern figures in San Francisco life, most notably the homeless and urban poor, by creating autonomous spaces that allowed homeless activists to democratically engage with one another. These spaces not only made the homeless visible but also empowered them to develop and deliver demands. This is a different form of empowerment that can occur through political inclusion and symbolic protest.

In addition, the struggle between Food Not Bombs on one side, and Agnos and the police on the other, underscores how intensified forms of control and regulation in public space becomes increasingly important for municipal governments to silence political dissent and depoliticize the poor and marginalized. Austerity economics and the securitization of public space exclude and silence. Thus public space is increasingly the site of contestation: occupying public spaces makes people not only *visible* but politically empowered. The violent and excessive crackdown of Occupy Wall Street protestors in November 2011 and Food Not Bombs activists in Orlando in July 2011 are examples of how city mayors and the political elites understand the fragility of neoliberal urban order. In repressing these movements cities use permits for health codes, noise ordinances, and parks to regulate and control radical social movements in public space. For movements that accept this form of government involvement, negotiated management means that their how, where, and when will be regulated in such a way as to limit their disruptive ability. Those groups that resist attempts at control and make autonomous claims in public spaces will most likely draw conflicts with government institutions.

Overall though, the narrative described throughout is positive, highlighting the ways that an activist group can, through the use of direct action and autonomous political claims, alter political relationships and recast public space in a major US city. In this case, Food Not Bombs, by overcoming the state's attempts to forcibly include the group into the state-charity nexus, made visible the structural violence of poverty and homelessness in San Francisco. Since most middle-class residents and visitors to the city did not want to be reminded of the destitute and poor, by empowering them, Food Not Bombs helped turn the homeless into political actors who pressured Agnos and other liberal/progressives in San Francisco through political mobilization and a politics of refusal. This, in effect, helped shatter Agnos's already precariously built coalition. In the end, it was not just party mobilization, political lobbying, or well-crafted media campaigns that broke apart this coalition and changed San Francisco's discourse on homelessness. It was about a small group of homelessness activists, making soup from discarded vegetables, and serving it for free in public space.

Notes

1 The last time the police in San Francisco harassed Food Not Bombs was a few months before the 2000 Mayoral election. According to long-time Food Not Bombs activist Chris Crass, the public outcry in the city was enormous and within a day all charges were dropped.

2 While to many, this autonomous desire might be seen as utopian and inherently problematic—echoing Simon Springer's reminder that democratically controlled public space is always on the precipice of disorder—it is an essential component of anarchist and radical homelessness politics. The desire for self-management is central to contemporary anarchist politics, as seen by contemporary anarchism's push for participatory workplaces, direct democratic political organizing, and cooperative living.

3 The Yerba Buena Center and the A-1and A-2 redevelopment plans of the 1970s radically altered the landscape of the city. These two plans changed the Mission district community by displacing thousands of Filipinos, as well as other immigrant communities, in order to build a new business center and shopping area. During the 1970s these plans were front and center in the struggle over gentrification in the city.

4 Through interviews I conducted with some of the early organizers, I learned that applying for the permit was a contentious issue that many in the group did not want to do; however, no one at the time thought that it was going to be an issue as far as the city was concerned.

5 Internal memos found in Art Agnos archives show that his administration was aware of the Cole Valley Association and had read their grievances with Food Not Bombs and responded.

6 This is the first time in Food Not Bombs' history that activists were arrested for distributing food. This became a sign of things to come, as many cities during the 1990s and 2000s targeted Food Not Bombs activists for arrest.

7 Even though Food Not Bombs rejected the logic of permits and rejected the authority of the state, they were also compelled to negotiate over permits. What is important to notice is that the more they transgressed, the more the state reacted with violence, but also the more willing the state was to concede to them around matters such as permit costs.

4

The war against the homeless: Frank Jordan, broken windows, and anti-homeless politics in San Francisco

There was a group of three homeless residents in Eugene, Oregon who would come to Food Not Bombs every Sunday, until June 2008. This group, which consisted of two men and a woman, made it to nearly every single meal. They would bring an appetite and funny stories, a lighthearted acceptance of the absurdity of life, and a political astuteness of how capitalism, police brutality, and militarism operated. While I was not incredibly close to this group of friends, I did know them, and I enjoyed being able to spend part of my Sunday afternoon talking to them. I remember the last conversation I had with them, largely because it was about the increased harassment they were receiving by the Eugene police force, as all three had received at least one ticket and been arrested in the space of a week. Then, just like that, they disappeared. This group of people, who had been sharing food and breaking bread with us for around a year, just vanished. The other homeless residents we knew had no idea what happened to them, but they all assumed that they fled, fearful of the coming police crackdown that was just around the corner.

These three friends were not the only homeless residents of Eugene who left the city due to increasing police harassment in the weeks leading up to the 2008 Olympic Track and Field Trials. Of course, the city made no claim that they were rounding up the homeless, but for those of us who either lived on the streets or regularly interacted with people who did, it was clear that the city had shifted its priorities. Most likely, the city realized that the trials represented a big opportunity for Eugene to make a good impression, and local leaders did not want the sizable homeless community detracting from the city's beauty or its vibrant and fun downtown extravaganzas. Much as we had witnessed in San Francisco, Eugene increased the amount of tickets and arrests for quality-of-life crimes throughout the city, and the homeless residents, unable to pay the ticket costs or get a lawyer to defend them, just left. In an era of precarity and neoliberal economic restructuring, tourists always matter more than local homeless residents. The market has spoken, and the poor have lost.

This chapter explores a much more coordinated and well-funded effort by the Frank Jordan administration against the homeless community in San Francisco. Jordan, who became mayor after defeating the then incumbent Art Agnos, did so, in large part, due to his tough on crime and tough on homelessness positions. After taking office, Jordan implemented one of the first large-scale quality-of-life and broken-windows police programs in the United States: the Matrix Program. This program primarily directed local police officers to follow a zero-tolerance policy around quality-of-life crimes—from drinking in public, to sleeping in public—combined with a series of mayor office support ballot initiatives that would reform GA benefits for the homeless and criminalized panhandling within the city. Referring to himself as the "Citizen Mayor" and the representative of real San Franciscans, Jordan's policies were self-described attempts to reclaim the city back from homeless residents who had stolen it. In a revanchist move, he turned the political struggle over space in San Francisco into a war to make the homeless suffer for the crime of being homeless.

This chapter focuses on the homeless program that Frank Jordan put in place during his term as mayor and contextualizes it within the broader theoretical work on space, visibility, and social control. It begins with an overview of Frank Jordan's homelessness politics and the theoretical ways that it dealt with space, power, citizenship, and economic development. From there the deeper theoretical underpinning of his project is explored, focusing first on the way that quality-of-life rhetoric and policies attempted to redefine San Francisco citizenship by turning the homeless into an anti-citizen, someone who needs to be excluded and oppressed for citizenship to have value. Secondly we will explore the ways that the Matrix program's policing and social service provisions worked to regulate, manage, and confine the homeless, primarily through physical coercion and a specific form of visibility, one that focuses on population data.

Statistics don't feel pain: Frank Jordan, the Matrix Quality of Life Program, and the war against the homeless

Voters elected Jordan because he said he would do something about anti-social spongers who flout the law, break the rules and degrade the quality of city life. It took a while, but with the dawn of Matrix, the Mayor has finally begun to deliver. (Saunders, 1993a)

Frank Jordan, who had been Agnos's first chief of police, was elected in 1991, in part due to his success at making the election a referendum on Agnos's failed homelessness policies. Agnos had campaigned to change the way the city addressed homelessness, but failed to address structural problems that caused homelessness. In addition, the growing resistance to his administration, by groups like Food Not Bombs, broke apart his coalition, making him seem draconian by the left and weak by the right. In response, Jordan ran as the tough on crime political outsider candidate, who was going to retake the city back from the homeless.

The architect of Jordan's homelessness policies was Kent Sims, Jordan's first Economic and Redevelopment director and the former president of the Economic Development Corporation, a non-profit think-tank that represented San Francisco business and tourism interests. Sims, in both his reports, *Homeless Problem* and "Homelessness in San Francisco" (MOEPD, 1992), states that San Francisco had become a magnet city for homeless people, and the only way to fix the problem was to stop the flow of homeless immigrants into the city. San Francisco attracted the poor because of its population density, which supported panhandling, and because of its liberal attitude and strong social service programs. He writes: "Currently our City has a self-proclaimed reputation as a sanctuary for for [*sic*] anyone who does not fit in elsewhere. We should make clear that our tolerance does not extend to those who come here principally for a welfare livelihood. We need to develop the reputation of a tough, not an easy place to be homeless" (McGarry, 2008: 180, italics added).

To change the city's magnetic appeal to homeless people, Sims argued that the city needed to: lower the visibility of the homeless (whose visual presence harms business and deters tourists from visiting); strongly enforce prohibitions on sleeping, drinking, and urinating in public; and decrease the quality and availability of the city's social services (McGarry, 2008: 165). By changing the discussion towards the inward flow of undesirable populations, Sims was able to deflect discussion away from the structural and institutional reasons for homelessness in San Francisco—from lack of affordable housing, to the decreasing salaries for most of the city's work force. He instead framed homelessness as the result of a rational cost-benefit calculation made by the homeless, who are mooching off the kindness of San Franciscans. He also redefined the homeless as immigrants to the community, and therefore not members of the community who deserve to be included and represented by government.

Sims also framed the homeless as people unable to help themselves because of mental health and addiction problems. Because of these problems, he contended that the homeless were irrational and that the city needed to deny them agency and political involvement. He argued that the city should treat the homeless paternalistically, limiting benefits but still providing them when doing so would help the city's economy, and punishing them aggressively otherwise. His overall claim was that a "fundamental problem with our city policy . . . has been that it reflects principally the interests of social services agencies and homeless advocates—rather than the needs and concerns of the larger non-homeless community of business and residents, and a realistic assessment of the needs of homeless people themselves" (McGarry, 2008: 179). In effect, he claimed that the homeless and their advocates had wrongfully taken over the city's politics and pushed policies that hurt the majority of San Franciscans. In a revanchist move, Sims called for Jordan to take the city back from the homeless advocates by decreasing the role of social service agencies and homeless non-governmental organizations in the policy process, and to then promote homeless policies that focused on the interests and needs of the business community.

During his entire term as mayor, Jordan concerned himself with erasing San Francisco's magnet reputation, by further criminalizing homelessness, and by sanitizing tourist and middle-class public spaces of homelessness. This was mostly done via Jordan's Matrix Quality of Life Program, a ground-breaking broken-windows policing policy. On paper, the Matrix plan was "a multi-departmental city effort to help people living on the streets obtain shelter and other services (such as psychiatric and drug and alcohol treatment), while at the same time protecting the general public from certain offenses committed in public" (Gardner and Lindstrom, 1997: 110). In reality, however, it was a police operation, which was characterized as "the most systematic, far-reaching criminal justice strategy ever devised by a San Francisco government (perhaps by any American municipal government) to control its ever-increasing homeless population" (Gardner and Lindstrom, 1997: 98).

The Matrix program enforced zero-tolerance quality-of-life laws concerning lodging in public, trespassing, public inebriation, willful and malicious obstruction, public consumption of alcohol, obstructing a sidewalk, remaining on private or business property, urinating or defecating in public, possession of a shopping cart, soliciting on or near a highway, sleeping in vehicles on the street, sleeping in public, erecting tends or structures in parks, obstructing a sidewalk with an object, and aggressive panhandling (Gardner and Lindstrom, 1997: 97). In the 15 months that the plan was enforced, approximately 39,000 citations or arrests were given, with nearly 50% being for public intoxication (McGarry, 2008: 232). In effect, nearly 40,000 citations and arrests were made in a city that has, on average, 10,000 homeless residents—i.e., on average, nearly four citations or arrests for each homeless resident in San Francisco during this 15-month period. The citations and arrests cost the homeless community approximately $3 million in penalties, an excessively large sum for a segment of the population shackled by extreme poverty, and cost the city nearly $10 million, including jail time and district attorney fees (Gardner and Lindstrom, 1997: 108).

The Matrix program had its start in a December 1992 police program that was designed to use community policing and neighborhood involvement to address serious crimes—burglaries, theft, and assault. In August 1993, mayor Jordan, in conjunction with police chief Anthony Ribera, decided to expand the program to include homelessness and quality-of- life crimes in high-traffic business and tourist areas of San Francisco—most notably in and around Civic Center Park and UN Plaza. That month, the plan was quietly implemented in the Tenderloin and Civic Center on a temporary basis. After that, the mayor and police chief proclaimed Matrix a success and decided to expand the program to include most major tourist and business sectors of the city.

After the first three months of Matrix being solely a police operation, the mayor's office expanded the program to include social service and housing agencies, but the social service arm was left woefully underfunded. According to a *San Francisco Weekly* report in 1995, Matrix only fully funded seven social workers to do housing and alcohol treatment outreach. Those seven social workers directed a little over 200 people to housing or drug referral programs in a six-month period, while nearly 22,000 people were cited for a criminal offense (Cothran, 1995). Social service benefits did not, overall, increase with the Matrix plan. For instance, alcohol and drug rehabilitation programs actually saw a decrease in clientele. Discussing the decrease in substance abuse referrals, Frank Spinelli of McMillan Drop In Center was quoted as saying, "I get a sense that police are being instructed to make arrests rather than offer detox options" (Granahl and Taylor, 1994).

Despite the woefully limited social service component to the program, the mayor commonly framed Matrix as an outreach program.[1] The *San Francisco Weekly*, in an article about the social service record of the Matrix plan, stated:

No one is faulting the outreach teams for their dismal record. In addition to Matrix, the city hosts some 20 outreach programs—most run by nonprofits—and they all face the same harsh reality: The number of homeless so overwhelms the city's bulwark of low-income housing, shelter and clinical services that street outreach is, at best, an exercise in wishful thinking. What irks advocates for the poor is that Jordan is bundling liberal programs developed long before he was elected and calling the amalgam "Matrix" in order to perpetuate the illusion that the homeless are well cared for. Rather than build a more effective system of government assistance, the Mayor and supervisors have cut social service budgets every year since 1992. (Cothran, 1995)

The statistics make clear the reality of Matrix, which Jordan upheld to existing social services as proof that the Matrix program was not entirely about police powers, but in truth social service programs were not expanded—the mayor actually cut funding for those services every year he was in office. Further, Jordan made social workers' jobs harder by forcing them to work more closely with the police.

In the summer of 1995, Jordan expanded the Matrix program under Matrix II, a plan to extend the current enforcement to the city's parks in outlying neighborhoods. This expansion occurred for two reasons. First, the mayor had been coming under political pressure, mostly from conservative developers and neighborhood associations, because the homeless were being dislocated from commercial districts and relocating to residential neighborhoods. The increase in homelessness within typically wealthy, white, and family-friendly neighborhoods threatened his political coalition (King and Bowman, 1994). Second, on August 19, 1995, a police dog was fatally shot and a police officer and three homeless park residents wounded by a homeless gunman residing in Golden Gate Park. After the shooting, the mayor announced that the city would strictly enforce a 10 p.m. ban on sleeping in city parks and the 500 to 1,000 residents of Golden Gate Park, in particular, would have to find a different place to sleep (Delgado, Winokur, & Allison, 1995; Levy, 1995; Rojas and Pimentel, 1995; Staff, 1995).

The first Matrix program centered on tourist and commercial districts of the city, which were places, Jordan argued, where homelessness had a significant effect on the tourist economy; the impact of this was that the homeless were pushed into the outskirts of the city and into the local parks. The expansion of Matrix into the parks and outlying residential neighborhoods was an attempt to further squeeze the homeless out of the community. The order of the campaign also highlights the logic behind the Matrix program. The first wave was to make it harder for the homeless to interact with tourists, but in doing so, the homeless where displaced from the city center to the local neighborhoods. The second round of actions attempted to do the same for local homeowners, and force the homeless into shelters or out of the city.

In addition to the Matrix program, the Jordan administration used the ballot system to expand its revanchist policies against the homeless and poor. Jordan relied on the ballot system, in large part, because he did not have a majority coalition on the board of supervisors and was limited in his executive power, which meant he had to find a way to expand his campaign against the homeless another way—direct appeals to the voters seemed to be the most effective approach. During his four years as mayor, his administration wrote and sponsored ten ballot initiatives, five of which dealt with homelessness and poverty issues. Of these five initiatives, four passed, most with overwhelming (more than 55%) support. These ballot initiatives included a 1992 aggressive panhandling ban (Proposition J), a GA

Proposition	Year	Goal	% Yes
J	1992	Ban aggressive panhandling	55
V	1993	Drastic welfare reform	61
J	1994	ATM boundary	58
M	1994	Ban obstructing a sidewalk	49
N	1994	Mandatory rent payment plan	51

4.1 Homelessness and poverty related ballot initiatives

reform initiative in 1993 (Proposition V), an ATM boundary law in 1994 (Proposition J), a 1994 ban on obstructing a sidewalk (Proposition M), and a mandatory rent payment plan in 1994 (Proposition N) (see figure 4.1).

Three of these ballot initiatives dealt directly with quality-of-life management—both the 1992 and the 1994 Proposition J and Proposition M, while the other two—Proposition V and Proposition N—were reforms of general assistance. The three quality-of-life policies are relatively straight-forward, as both propositions that passed criminalized further an action commonly associated with the homeless—panhandling—while the proposal that went beyond the homeless, blocking a sidewalk, was defeated in large part due to opposition from civil rights organizations and broader fears of limiting free speech on public sidewalks (Lynch, 1993: A30).

The two general assistance reform initiatives—Proposition V and Proposition N—addressed access to GA funds. Proposition V drastically reformed the GA procedure, most notably by mandating the fingerprinting of recipients and increasing the requirements for entrance into the program. The city saw fingerprinting as a way to quickly check criminal records of assistance recipients, giving authorities access to records in San Francisco and surrounding cities. The proposed reason for the plan was to root out GA frauds who came to San Francisco to get money but lived elsewhere. According to the mayor, because this proposal was to root out fraud, Proposition V made it harder to get GA benefits in San Francisco, requiring a 15-day proof of residence within the city. By the end of Jordan's tenure as mayor, only 200 homeless residents had lost access to city-funded GA due to these new loopholes. There is no data available, however, on how many people who had been eligible for funding did not apply due to the lengthy and invasive new requirements that the city imposed. The law also did not even come close to addressing its primary stated objective—to save the city money—as costs associated with implementing it drastically limited the real dollar amount, saving the city well under a million dollars a year, even though it had estimates of saving approximately 1.2 million dollars a year (McGarry, 2008: 282–283).

The second GA benefits-related program was the mandatory rent payment plan, or Proposition N. Proposition N required all homeless GA recipients to accept an open SRO hotel room if one was available, in exchange for a significant decrease in their GA financial support. This plan was seen as an alteration of the long-running volunteer rent payment plan, which allowed homeless residents in the city to decide if they wanted to accept an SRO in exchange for part of their monthly benefits. Of course most of the SRO hotels were substandard and, in effect, the city would be subsidizing the slumlords who ran these hotels (Levy, 1994). This all said, even though Proposition N passed, the board of supervisors actively blocked its implementation, effectively killing the program until it was rebranded as "care not cash" by Gavin Newsome, and then passed in 2001.

Although both the new policies for GA benefits and the Mandatory Rent Payment Plan were marketed as ways of lowering government costs and rooting out fraud, the primary impacts of both policies were much more nefarious. First off, the new policies marked a strong move away from Agnos's liberal state-centered approach to homelessness—which, while problematic, was influenced by progressive values around providing government support for the homeless—towards a much more neoliberal understanding of homelessness politics. These proposals sought to label the homeless individuals as potential causes for the city's problem, characterizing them as welfare cheats and as irresponsible and irrational market actors, with the Mandatory Rent Payment plan. Echoing Kent Sims, Jordan asserted that large amounts of GA money were being spent on drugs and alcohol, which went hand in hand with the administration's claim that the majority of homeless people were on the streets because of addiction problems. The Jordan administration argued that it was foolish to allow people, who are either addicts or mentally ill, to have free reign on spending their own money. Instead, the city had to make sure that they were good homeless worthy of government support and aid, and then paternalistically limit their choices around housing and the spending of their own money. Secondly, both the quality-of-life and GA reform propositions and the Matrix program attempted to increase the costs of being homeless in San Francisco. These policies can be seen as the primary ways that the city tried to change the supposed magnet image of San Francisco, as a place supportive of the homeless and poor. These proposals increased the cost of homelessness in the city by making it significantly harder to get access to social services, lowering the value of the social services that were available, by drastically increasing the likelihood of citations and arrests, and by forcibly removing the homeless from parts of the city seen as central to the tourist industry and wealthy residents' happiness. The program was partially successful in displacing San Francisco's homeless population, especially from central business and tourist locale, as cities such as Berkley and Oakland saw notable increases in their homeless populations. Police Lt. Dennis Martel said, regarding the displacement of the homeless: "If people are now finding they can't do whatever they want here, and that makes them uncomfortable, then that is good news" (Lynch, 1993: A30). These two impacts are not contradictory but are actually mutually reinforcing components of the city's move towards a neoliberal management of homelessness. The city needed to increase surveillance and regulation of its homeless residents, to deny them access to government resources, and to shift the administration of these programs from the government to private businesses, such as the owners of SRO hotels; and they did so by appealing to city residents' economic concerns.

In the next section, we will go deeper into Jordan's political program and explore the theoretical logic and implications of the Matrix program and its impact on the homeless community. The first part of the next section will explore the ways in which the revanchist policies of the Jordan administration attempted to restructure the political community in such a way as to exclude the homeless as political subjects, effectively making them anti-citizens. The second section explores the ways in which the state used government-enforced visibility—through policing and social services—as a way of containing and regulating the homeless community. Essentially, the process of making them visible to the state was a tool to make them invisible to the rest of the political public.

Redefining the political community: the homeless and anti-citizenship

In expanding the neoliberalization of homelessness in San Francisco, the Jordan administration politically shifted the discussion of homelessness and the homeless. During the Agnos administration (and before) the homeless were viewed as people in desperate need of government support and assistance. In effect, the Agnos administration viewed them through a lens of pity. With Jordan, the city shifted to a politics of revanchism. Neil Smith, in his groundbreaking book on gentrification, *The new urban frontier: gentrification and the revanchist city*, argues that the wave of gentrification in the 1980s turned into the revanchist urban politics of the 1990s. By revanchist, Smith refers to:

> a political movement that formed in France in the last three decades of the nineteenth century. Angered by the increased liberalism of the Second Republic, the ignominious defeat of Bismarck, and the last straw—the Paris Commune (1870–1871), in which the Paris working class vanquished the defeated government of Napoleon III and held the city for months—the revanchists organized a movement of revenge and reaction against both the working class and the discredited royalty. . . . It was a right-wing movement built on populist nationalism and devoted to a vengeful and reactionary retaking of the country. (Smith, 1996: 45)

According to Smith, the modern revanchist movement is comprised of middle-class, white city residents who feel that, due to urban liberal politics from the New Deal to Ronald Reagan, their cities have been stolen from them. They've been stolen by minorities, gays and lesbians, immigrant groups, and the homeless. The revanchists sought to take back the city through reactionary policies that would punish those perceived to be the thieves.

The rise of revanchist policies in the 1990s, according to Smith, represents a shift and change in gentrification policy. While the 1980s saw city officials using city money to fund gentrification efforts, the 1990s approach was to use the police and social services agencies to make the urban environment pro-business. This shift was accomplished by punishing those who hurt business—the poor, the non-white, and the homeless.

Frank Jordan can be understood as one of the first revanchist mayors in the United States. The self-described Citizen Mayor wanted to represent all San Franciscans and not social workers and homeless activists. In effect, Jordan defined himself as representing those voices and interests that had been shut out of City Hall since the rise of urban liberalism in the 1960s. His goal was to reclaim the city for these "original" San Franciscans, who had been pushed, by homeless residents, out of the parks, tourist areas, and sidewalks. The homeless, to Jordan, represented a group of addicted and mentally ill folks who were invading the city from outside (the flow problem) and needed to be punished for engaging in antisocial behavior. Revanchism was at the root of Jordan's homelessness policy, which cut social services, increased police harassment, and decreased the already limited autonomy and agency of homeless residents.

Jordan's revanchism was built on neoconservative broken-windows policing. Much like Giuliani in New York, Jordan dealt with homelessness and social problems by using the police and targeting categories of people who are defined as burdens on the city. The goal was to decrease the amount of money spent on social services, sanitize the public space of social deviants and signs of disorder, and reclaim the city with a vengeance. Jordan rejected the structural or institutional causes of homelessness, arguing that homelessness was largely the fault of individuals, and, more importantly, that the homeless were a threat to the social, economic, and political order, thus the city needed to punish those whose bad choices harmed the whole.

To forge a revanchist politics, Jordan had to clearly delineate the limits of the San Francisco political community, defining the real San Franciscans in an attempt to construct an enemy/friend distinction between the real citizens and the threatening other. In doing this, Frank Jordan constructed the homeless, and their political accomplices, as the enemy of the public good, and promoted a politics of reclaiming political power from these forces who had illegitimately wielded power during the Agnos administration.

Discursively this was the basis of both the Matrix program and GA reforms. In the administration's own language, these programs were described as a way to take back the city for middle-class residents, businesses, and tourists, and improve their quality of life. Following the intellectual work by Sims, who defined the administration's ideological project, the government believed that the homeless and their allies had an illegitimate and unreasonable amount of power over policy, and that business interests and homeowners were excluded. As the *San Francisco Chronicle* stated: "Jordan is seeking nothing less than to toughen a city that he claims has been taken advantage of." Further highlighting this are the words of Jordan aide Bill Wunderman, who stated "We are not turning our backs on the needy. But people are tired of seeing things in this city go downhill, and there are certain things we won't accept anymore" (McGarry, 2008: 276).[2] Lastly, an anonymous mayor's aide told the *San Francisco Chronicle*, "Public patience has worn out ... We want to take back the parks, automatic teller machines, alleys, the streets, our plazas, our playgrounds for all citizens" (McGarry, 2008: 277). By framing parks, streets, and public spaces as being occupied by a small section of the city causing detriment to the public, Jordan attempted to construct an oppositional politics that pitted the homeless against the rest of the public. But he did not just describe the homeless as negative to businesses; the administration also made a deeper argument about the existential nature of the homeless, arguing that they were not fit to be citizens either.

The logical underpinning of Sims' and Jordan's understanding of the homeless contradictorily argues that the homeless are rational actors seeking benefits and handouts, while at the same time irrational and irresponsible, so therefore should be denied personal autonomy, the right to make economic choices, or the ability to be political actors. This contradictory view of the homeless in San Francisco is not new; it is a re-emerging theme that has its origins in the cultural movement against vagrants and transients, following the enclosure of the commons in Europe. The vagrant figures displaced by the enclosures were defined as both taking advantage of the nascent capitalist economic system and irrationally acting as a threat against it. As Foucault highlights in his lectures *On The Punitive Society*, displaced people during the enclosure movements were seen as a threat to the newly forming capitalist economic order. Foucault states that:

If we stick to these first three effects of vagabondage, we see that the vagabond is no longer someone who takes part of consumption without working, as he was in the Middle Ages. He is not so much someone who attacks the mass of things to be consumed, as someone who attacks the mechanism of production ... The vagabond is therefore someone who disrupts production and not just a sterile consumer. He therefore occupies a position of constitutive hostility with regard to the normal mechanism of production. (Foucault, Harcourt, & Burchell, 2015: 47)

As official threats to the system of production, the vagabond was seen as being at war with society and as such their enslavement, death, and re-education was a necessary process to make society whole again. The vaga-bond, as an irrational actor, had to be destroyed, and the system had to be changed to make it less likely for individuals to rationally become vaga-bonds in the first place. In a similar way, the homeless in San Francisco were positioned as an existential threat to the economic order of the city, by refusing to engage as respectable neoliberal subjects and rationally using the generosity of the state against itself.

In constructing the homeless as the enemy of the citizens of San Fran-cisco, Jordan politically marginalized the homeless, giving them pariah status, and in effect making them anti-citizens, or political subjects that serve as an other that helps to define what it means to be a citizen. If the liberal citizen is defined as rational, economic, self-regulating, social, and predictable, the narrative developed by Sims and others within the Jordan administration was to view the homeless as their opposite: irrational, non-economic, impulsive, anti-social, and irresponsible. This discursively worked to symbolically remove them from the political community by denying them the essential features of citizenship.

In the US context, citizenship and membership of the political community has always been defined racially. According to Joel Olson (2004), this is because the American democratic system emerges with slavery, and, in fact, slavery for blacks was central for white democratic freedoms. Olson argues that in the US context, blackness has historically served as a form of anti-citizenship that was used to define what it meant to be a citizen, and thus black Americans were perennial outsiders, never able to be fully incorpo-rated into US citizenship.

The anti-politics around homelessness is linked to this longer history of white supremacy. If you look at the history of homelessness in the United States, late eighteenth-century vagrants, who tended to be newly freed black slaves forced into vagrancy due to economic conditions, had to endure a range of white paternalistic practices. The primary disciplinary institution they interacted with were poorhouses. Much like the Native American boarding schools, the poorhouses were seen as spaces to impose what was considered white values (hard work, puritanical morality, and rationality) on non-white communities that were deemed not to have these traits. The racist paternalism at play allowed the poorhouses to require residents to go through religious education classes and engage in a manual labor exchange for food and shelter. Because homelessness was linked to race, even whites who were homeless during the nineteenth and early twentieth century were racialized and viewed more as blacks than as good, god-fearing Christians.

The poorhouse solution to homelessness was to reform the homeless, and, through the process of religious education and forced labor, make them white, or at least white enough not to be deemed a threat to the state.

As Craig Willse (2015) mentions, during the Great Depression the cultural view of houselessness shifted away from being only a personal problem, and instead became a structural problem that required massive government support to address. What is important to note about this period, however, is that this was the first time in US history in which a large number of the houseless were displaced whites. The racial makeup cannot be understated—especially since US history has regularly filtered people, depending on their race, into different types of social services. Historically, white labor and communities have had access to well-regarded and destigmatized federal government programs (like social security, Medicare, or the GI bill), while non-white communities have been filtered into either stigmatized federal programs (public housing and Medicaid) or state-run social services (food stamps and welfare). As Willse argues, "Federalism became the governance apparatus that could simultaneously serve the state-building demands of welfare policy and the race hierarchy building of US white supremacy" (Willse, 2015: 39–40). The racialized treatment of homelessness and housing was central to this project, as it allowed the "public to invest in the health and well-being of only part of the population and still solidify the nation" (Willse, 2015: 39). When it comes to homelessness, the success of the 1950s and 1960s white New Deal meant that the large numbers of white homeless disappeared and the remaining could be viewed as abnormal race traitors mired in addiction, mental illness, or poor life choices. Either way, in the 1980s and 1990s, homelessness, once again, became dominantly viewed through a racial lens.

This leads us to understand the shift in San Francisco, with Jordan, to construct the homeless as the primary other of the San Francisco citizenship. In the 1991 election, while homelessness was not the only topic of coverage, it was one of the primary differences between Jordan and the other candidates in the ballot. As the *New York Times* contextualized the 1991 election "Panhandlers seem to be multiplying on downtown street corners. There is litter by the curbs and graffiti on the buses. Polls show that residents of San Francisco are running out of patience with the homeless and that suburbanites consider this a dirty, dangerous city and are staying away" (Markell, 1991).[3] Jordan staked his position as the "Mayor for all San Franciscans," contrasting the real San Franciscan with a nomadic, and potentially newly immigrated, homeless figure. In an ad Jordan's campaign produced, well-known San Francisco landmarks—from the Golden Gate Bridge, Fisherman's Wharf, and the curvy Lombard street—are portrayed with their views blocked by black-and-white pictures of homeless people. The meaning of this ad is clear: black bodies darken and make unsafe an otherwise beautiful picture of San Francisco. This perspective was also central to Sim's discourse of homelessness as being a form of migration, which shares much in common with white nationalist fears of an immigrant invasion. To Sims, the magnet-nature of San Francisco means the city is being inundated with outsiders who are abusing the generosity of the San Franciscan. By decreasing the services provided and making them significantly harder to attain, the home-less would self-deport themselves from San Francisco—decreasing the burden on the San Francisco citizens. Discursively, this argument denies the homeless membership of the local community—they are not citizens or residents who happen to be houseless, they are instead threats and burdens to the citizen—who is therefore defined as a housed individual. In effect, the defining feature of citizenship in this digressive operation is not length of residency within the city, but instead access to housing, which, in turn, made tourists residents of the city, while the homeless were systemically excluded.

Police batons and social workers: social control and the Matrix program

The homeless not only served as a mean of defining who is, and is not, a member of the political community, they were also turned into a social threat. As Foucault argues, crime and disorder become increasingly tied to issues of social war during the seventeenth and eighteenth century, and criminals ceased to be just immoral figures, but enemies engaging in civil war with the capitalist, Christian, state. The same process was at play with Jordan, the former police chief, between the city and the homeless commu-nity. The struggle between Jordan and the homeless had two prongs. Fist, via the coercive power of the police and, secondly, via the informational and soft power wielded by the social service agencies. The primary goal of both institutions was to contain, control, and manage the homeless community.

During the three years that the city ran the Matrix program, approxi-mately 39,000 quality-of-life citations were issued to members of the home-less community, so an average of 13,000 citations a year. This, in a city with approximately 15,000 homeless, means that there were nearly as many citations as there were homeless residents. This 13,000-a-year citation number is significantly higher than during the Agnos administration where, according to a report compiled by the San Francisco Coalition for the Homeless, the city never exceeded 8,000 citations in any given year. Since citations and tickets tended to be unpayable by homeless residents, they quickly turned into warrants for arrest and many of the cited homeless ended up spending time in prison, effectively, losing access to government support programs like GA and food stamps.

That said, the citations were not uniformly issued throughout the city, but seemed to be targeted in specific locations, following the logic of containment during the black plague, where certain spaces of a city need to be quarantined to protect the flow of disease from spreading throughout the city (Foucault, 1995). The logic underpinning the plague quarantine was that if a carrier of plague gets into a healthy part of the city, the disease can spread, harming political order and economic efficiency. A similar logic was applied in San Francisco to the homeless, as Sims and mayor Jordon saw homelessness as a plague that hurt the economic and social order of the city. The homeless, then, like the leper and the plague barrier of old, needed to be quarantined and kept away from certain parts of the city—largely tourist centers and newly gentrified neighborhoods. This cordoned the city in such a way that certain areas became defined as acceptable for the homeless to exist within, while others were not. By pushing the homeless away from tourist locations and out of newly gentrifying parts of the city, the effect was to barricade the homeless within the Tenderloin, where the majority of homeless services were provided, and protect the rest of the city from them.

In attempting to limit homeless access to the majority of the city, especially the tourist and wealthier areas, the mayor's office attempted to decrease the ability of the homeless in the city to subsidize their government assistance via panhandling, which was even further limited by the passage of anti-panhandling laws in 1994. At the same time, by coordinating the homeless into one part of town, it became easier to police, monitor and regulate that community and to decrease their disruption to the larger economic flows of goods and services within the city.

The attempted exclusion of the homeless from specific parts of the city had two broad impacts. First, with the exclusion of the homeless from wealthy and tourist areas, they could be made invisible to both groups. Secondly, by decreasing the presence of the homeless from certain public spaces, the city was attempting to decrease the political power and voice that homeless residents of the city had developed during the Agnos administration. This is because, as expressed in chapter 3, for marginalized groups their presence in public space was often the only way to engage the public and express their political existence. For the homeless, under Agnos, public occupation of space was one of their lasts grasps on making themselves members of the broader political public—especially in their tent-city in front of City Hall—and Jordan's attempt to crack down on the homeless community can be seen as an attempt to learn from his predecessor, albeit unsuccessfully, as we shall see in the next chapter.

In effect, the use of police force to contain the homeless within certain segments of the city was a means to limit homeless residents' ability to survive by making being homeless significantly harder. For instance, the use of citations, which inevitably turned into warrants, provided a way to sweep streets, if need be, and also forced many homeless residents to self-deport to places like Oakland, Berkeley, or Portland. The arrests also served as a way to enter people into the larger informational system, which, as we will see next, served as a tool of social control as well. Finally, the attempt to contain the homeless in the tenderloin also made panhandling, recycling, and other practices that they used to supplement their limited assistance, harder, putting additional, economic, pressure on the homeless to relocate to other, less aggressive, cities on the west coast.

In tandem with the physical coercion of the police, the city used its social services and social workers as an additional tool to manage and regulate the homeless community. Much like the prison, the school, and the work-place serve as tools for creating docile bodies (Foucault, 1995), the social service wing of the city was structured to regulate and control the homeless. As mentioned in the previous section, part of the large Matrix program included the employment of a small number of social workers, who pro-vided legitimacy for the program, disproving that it was only a policing operation, but who also served as a way to shuffle the visible homeless off the streets and into the social service wing of the city. This might seem to be acceptable at first glance, but combined with the increasing amount of surveillance, monitoring, and policing that become central to social service provisions within San Francisco during the Jordan administration, in effect the social workers and service providers became an arm of the larger war against the homeless.

There are two ways that the social service side of the Matrix programs served as a tool of repression to the homeless community. First, by funneling the homeless into social services, the city was able to increase the overall amount of data and information it had about members of this community. As Foucault and many others have argued, data is not inherently neutral but can, depending on the way the data is generated and used, serve as a tool to reinforce specific distributions of power. In this case, the data gener-ated were being used by a mayoral administration primarily interested in removing the homeless from public space. By turning the homeless into a generalizable population that can be managed, the social services of the state embraced the logic of neoliberal governmentality, which seeks to manipulate populations, via different incentive and disincentive structures, in order to ensure economic and political stability.

Beyond just generating and collecting data, due to the new policy shifts with the GA reforms and the increased dependence of the homeless on state support, the social service providers used their ability to provide limited access to housing, food, and social services as a way to incentivize certain behaviors and discourage others. Increasing the costs and barriers to gaining social services in the city primarily did this. The GA reforms, discussed earlier, collectively increased the cost to access services, required fingerprinting, actively removed people with criminal records from the GA roles, and then mandated that they move into an SRO room or a homeless shelter in order to receive any assistance, which was then lowered to cover the cost of that room. By funneling from the streets to the social service providers, the city was able to increasingly filter the homeless into good and bad homeless, provide housing for the good homeless, and force the bad homeless onto the streets where they dealt with a continuous cycle of arrests, warrants, and violence. This filtering process not only provided a justification for the police to crack down on the homeless, but the inclusion of service providers allowed the city to claim to be helping the homeless, decreased the city costs of services by shifting them to the police and court system, and removed the good homeless from public view, therefore working to exclude the homeless from the public sphere and creating the illusion of order.

Overall, the argument here is that the Matrix program attempted a two-pronged project against the homeless. First, it attempted to define the homeless through the lens of anti-citizenship, which meant that the homeless were not just excluded from politics but also became a pariah to the maintenance of the social order. Constructing homelessness this way allowed the city to have a war against the homeless, in which the state used its power to employ counter insurgent strategies against them. This meant the regulation of their population into specific areas via physical coercive force and also to use the power of social workers and state agencies to monitor and regulate them through the control of information. This was a partially failed war against the homeless, as homeless activists with Food Not Bombs and other groups organized successfully against the tactics employed by the Jordan administration. As the section below will highlight, Food Not Bombs resisted the city by reclaiming and occupying political space in strategic ways.

Conclusion

The Jordan administration's approach to homelessness was to perceive it as a social threat that had the potential to undermine the city's economic, political, and social stability. The homeless, cited as existential threats, meant that Jordan was unable to view them as people—with cares, wants, and emotions—and instead understood them only in the abstract—as a population variable in economic data reports. In turning to his background as a police chief, Jordan and his administration orchestrated a massive policing campaign to end homelessness. In seeing homelessness as a criminal issue, and the homeless as making a lifestyle choice, Jordan refused to acknowledge the largest systemic issues that feed into a crisis around houselessness. During his administration, there were massive cuts to affordable housing programs, along with increases in urban displacement and gentrification, and, as already stated, massive gutting of the city's social service agencies. Jordan instead relied on a network of private charities and police agencies to address homelessness in the city, neither of which addressed structural causes but instead focused, primarily, on individual choice as the cause of homelessness.

Jordan's homelessness policies were not really centered on ending homelessness, but, conversely, on removing the homeless from his city. In other words, the goal was the massive displacement of San Francisco's homeless community to other parts of the bay and the rest of the country. In order to increase the cost of homelessness and have the homeless self-deport from the city, the mayor waged a war against them. First, the mayor's office attempted to alter the discursive meaning of citizenship in San Francisco, in order to exclude the homeless as members of the broader community. He did this by pitting business owners, homeowners, and tourists (the real San Franciscans) against the homeless. The second prong was police operations to forcibly exclude them from parts of the city and, through arrests and social services, get them into the social services system.

These two methods of attack—discursive and coercive—needed to be implemented together because there is a strong linkage between public space and political space. As was mentioned in chapter 3, theorists of democratic space have argued that existence within public space provides a means for marginalized groups to become political actors; to disrupt and to make political demands. Because of this, Jordan needed to remove the homeless from public space in order to discursively remove them from the city's political space Of course, by making public space the locus of homeless struggles, Jordan opened up a space for resistance that groups like Food Not Bombs used to undermine his administration's policies. The next chapter explores Food Not Bombs' resistance to Jordan's Matrix program and his administration more generally. Central to their political campaign was the occupation and reclaiming of public space and an attempt to turn visibility into a tool of political liberation.

Notes

1 Tangentially related, in August and September the Mayor also proposed that the police start confiscating shopping carts from the homeless. In exchange for the shopping carts the city was planning to provide homeless residents with free duffle bags, donated by downtown businesses, and as many garbage bags as they needed. The belief was that cart removal would clean up the streets and save grocery stores thousands of dollars a year (Lynch 1993). But the cart plan came in for almost unanimous condemnation. Even columnist and pro-Matrix conservative Debra Saunders criticized the Mayor's plan. She claimed, "The guys with shopping carts aren't the reason you avoid the cable

car turnaround. Why pick on these guys?" (Saunders 1993b). In the end the Mayor toned down the rhetoric on shopping carts, asking grocery stores to increase their security instead.

2 Jordan's ballot plans, especially his GA reforms, also highlight the biopolitical nature of contemporary politics. With these reforms, Jordan claimed that the homeless and poor should not be viewed as having any form of political agency and instead should be regulated in much the same way that cities regulate public health and order problems. By viewing people as something to be contained to ensure the free flow of the economy, Jordan's policies illustrate the ways in which city governments, not just the federal and state government, engage in biopolitics.

3 www.nytimes.com/1991/08/26/us/san-francisco-Mayor-in-tough-bid-for-re-election.html.

5

The homeless fight back: the politics of homeless resistance

While I was rummaging through the San Francisco Coalition for the Homeless office, I saw a flier that said, "It only takes 5000 people to start a revolution . . . there are 15,000 homeless in San Francisco. Let's get organized." Eyeball deep in newspapers and newsletters, this flier was a reminder of the power of the homeless in urban spaces throughout the nation. Far too many of us have learned to block the homeless out of our minds, erasing them from our vision (often with the help of government policies), and walking over them instead of engaging with them, but the truth is that they have a political power that is not recognized. Since the 1980s there has been a concerted push by the bigger cities in the US to disempower the homeless, to make them publicly invisible, and turn them from political actors into urban weeds and broken windows that need fixing. But as anyone who has studied protests and politics knows, attempts to disempower people are almost always met by resistance. This chapter is about that exact resistance and the struggle of the homeless and their allies to fight back against the wave of anti-homeless laws and policies promoted by the Frank Jordan administration.

In resisting the city's attempts to further marginalize and remove the homeless, Food Not Bombs confronted the mayor nearly every place he went—from work, to home, to fundraising dinners. Protesting activists became the backdrop to his daily life. Every single day, the group would provide free meals, up to three a day, to homeless residents right in front of City Hall at the Civic Center Park and UN Plaza Park. This meant that at least three times a day, the mayor could look out of his office window and see a line of homeless, and their allies, eating and serving free food right in the heart of downtown. The battle between the two was not just waged in those parks, however, as Food Not Bombs activists would disrupt Frank Jordan's re-election benefits by protesting outside them, occupy the mayor's office and City Hall, and a few times even hold public meals in front of his house.

While Food Not Bombs activists were occupying public space in the heart of downtown and disrupting Frank Jordan's daily schedule, the mayor was fighting back, using the entire power of the city to do so. During his tenure as mayor, Jordon urged the police to crack down on Food Not Bombs activists, arresting them for any infraction they could; there was ample public speculation that the mayor's office was illegally surveilling Keith McHenry and other major figures within the group. During the four years of Frank Jordan's mayoral administration, over 700 arrests and citations were handed out by the police against the group. The massive amount of city harassment of the group prompted Amnesty International to come out in support of the activists, threatening to label them "prisoners of conscious" unless Jordan stopped his campaign. In their letter they wrote that:

> Amnesty International is concerned that the Food Not Bombs activists may have been targeted on account of their beliefs and effectively prohibited from exercising their right to freedom of expression, assembly, and the right to impart information. If this were found to be the case, the City of San Francisco would be in breach of international law and Amnesty International would adopt those imprisoned as "Prisoners of Conscience" and work for their unconditional release. (Amnesty International, 1994)

Though the group was never labeled as "prisoners of conscious," the fact that Amnesty even threatened to label them as such highlights the massive amount of government harassment the group was subjected to.

While Jordan's arrests had a profound impact on the group, making it harder for them to engage in activism, and costing thousands in lawyer's fees, the technique backfired on the mayor. If anything, the harassment meant that the group, and Jordan's homeless policies, where front and center in all conversations about city politics. This provided an opportunity, which the group took advantage of, to shape the framing and discussion around the mayor's homelessness politics within the city. Also, by occupying public space and not ceding ground to city officials, the group also undermined Jordan's attempt to regulate and maintain control over space. Since he linked the visibility of public order with power, Food Not Bombs effectively undermined Jordan's legitimacy with his supporters, making him a one-term mayor.

This chapter details Food Not Bombs' resistance to Frank Jordan's Matrix program, paying special attention to the daily meal services and the group's public occupation of UN Plaza during the 50th anniversary for the United Nations. Before detailing the history of resistance, we will first delve into an important theoretical discussion of what Food Not Bombs did, focusing on how, according to Jacques Rancière, they engaged in politics, and how, following Eduardo Glissant, they embraced a right to opacity and weaponized visibility. These ideas will provide insight into understanding the nature of resistance that occurred.

Politics and disruption

The previous chapter explored the many ways in which the Frank Jordan administration used the power of the state and the media pulpit to target the homeless. In his campaign for quality-of-life policies in San Francisco, he attempted to position the homeless as the enemy outsider, the threat to the body politic. In exploring and attempting to understand the resistance to Jordan's attempts, it is best to think of this fight as a dialectic between the city and the homeless activists fighting back for the definition of what it meant to be a political actor in San Francisco.

The political thinker who provides the strongest political analysis for the sort of dialectic of politics and political inclusion that happened in San Francisco is the French theorist Jacques Rancière, in his influential short piece "Ten Thesis on Politics." Rancière highlights the importance of understanding that all essential political categories are not pre-political and that each and every one is forged within a political and social struggle. This is especially true when it comes to concepts like citizenship and the people. It is important to remember that both these categories are defined, as Carl Schmitt points out, in contrast to their outside. So the citizen is defined by the non-citizen; the people by their enemy. The boundary between the two sides, however, is neither natural nor stable, but constantly in flux. Rancière reminds us of the original meaning of democracy, which holds that there should be "the complete absence of any entitlement to government" (Rancière, 2010: 31). But in the world of real existing government systems, there are limitations on who can, and cannot, govern. This is part of what he means when, in another work, he claims that the modern world has a "hatred of democracy" (Rancière, 2009). One of the primary goals of the modern state has been to restrict people's access to control the institutions that structure and govern their lives, often done via forced exclusion from the polls.

In "Ten Thesis," Rancière primarily defines the political landscape into two competing social forces: *police* and *politics*. The police are the forces of the status quo, the entity that is trying to maintain the current order. He argues "The essence of the police lies neither in repression nor even in the sensible. Its essence lies in a certain way of dividing up the sensible" (Rancière, 2010: 36). By dividing up the sensible, Rancière is talking about both the division and construction of the public and private spheres of life, and the construction of citizen and non-citizen. In effect, the police are there to enforce and, well, police the boundaries between constructed categories. Or to put it in simpler terms: to exclude. He writes that, "Traditionally, in order to deny the political quality of a category—workers, women, and so on—all that was required was to assert that they belonged to a 'domestic' space that was separated from public life" (Rancière, 2010: 38). This separation of public and private, as being central in defining the category of who should be included, clearly connects to the attempts by Jordan and others to exclude the homeless—who only exist in the public, and therefore bring the private (sexual relations, eating, sleeping, defecating, etc.) into the public. It is also important to note that Jordan used the homeless' existence in public space as an argument for the city to be a paternalistic figure, guiding and punishing them. Because the homeless live in public they must be treated as children and excluded from being political actors. This is the policing of the exclusion line, by the state in San Francisco.

The other side of Rancière's dialectic is *politics*. "The essence of politics," writes Rancière, "consists in disturbing this arrangement [the policing of exclusion] by supplementing it with a part of those without part, identified with the whole of the community . . . Politics, before all else, is an intervention in the visible and the sayable" (Rancière, 2010: 36–67). To put it in simpler terms, Rancière is arguing that *politics* is about breaking down the borders that the *police* enforce and therefore radically opening and changing the nature of inclusion and exclusion in a political community. This is why later in the article he claims, "The essence of politics is dissensus" (Rancière, 2010: 38). Why dissensus? Because the *police* are about constructing and maintaining a consensus, which he describes as "the reduction of politics to the police" (Rancière, 2010: 42), while *politics* alters this calculation and throws the political community into flux. This flux opens up space for a radical reimaging of the political community and is part of the long and arduous process for increased inclusion into the political community. In Rancière's work "consensus is 'the end of politic'" and dissensus its existence (Rancière, 2010: 42).

Bringing this back to the struggle in San Francisco between the Jordan administration and Food Not Bombs (and other radical homeless activists) the work of Rancière provides insight into the contested nature of defining and constructing a political community. He reminds us that these terms are not natural or pre-political, but a product of a dialectic between the forces of inclusion and exclusion, between consensus and dissensus. The last chapter saw the force of the *police*—the mayor, the police officers, and city agencies—that worked to exclude the homeless from the political community; this chapter shows the other side of the dialectic, *the politics* expressed by activists fighting back by reclaiming public space, forcing themselves into political discussions and the like. The disruptive power of the homeless was an essential component of their relative success and, as such, you can see their acts of resistance as being the defining characteristic of *politics*. It was through the process of resisting that the homeless both made themselves political agents and attempted to undermine a political consensus—both neoliberalism and broken-windows policing—which denied their political existence. Of course, just because you disrupt and fight does not mean that you are going to win, or going to undermine the dominant consensus, but it does remind us that there is no possibility for radical change, or the breakdown of the governing consensus, outside disruptive politics.

Opacity, visibility, and weaponizing public space

The previous chapter discussed the ways in which the state, under Jordan, turned the visibility of the homeless into a weapon for the state. The group, following Foucault's logic of governmentality, attempted to catalog, categorize, and manipulate the homeless population. In addition, the state attempted to quarantine the homeless within certain places, excluding them from others. Combined, this represents the state managing the homeless for the good of capital—to allow a free flow of tourists and money to circulate throughout the city. In this section, I want to complicate the nature of public space and make an argument that visibility, when used by the state, can be a form of coercive violence, when it is combined with an expanded version of what Eduardo Glissant calls the right to opacity.

Glissant, a post-colonial Caribbean poet and theorist, in a short section of his work *Poetics of relation* (1997), provides a quick analysis of the opacity and its relationship to post-colonial theory and politics. In this short section, he gives a powerful defense for the right to opacity by contrasting it to the Western demand for transparency. "If we examine the process of understanding people and ideas from the perspective of Western thought," Glissant writes, "we discover that its basis is this requirement for transparency" (Glissant, 1997: 190). This idea of making everything available and knowable is, from the Western perspective, essential in knowing the other. But this approach is unaware that the acceptance of difference, found in the politics of full transparency, ignores and hides hierarchies of power, and thus can serve as a form of coercive violence. In the decades since Glissant's work, many of the decolonial scholars—most notably Walter Mignolo (2011) in *The darker side of western modernity*—have contended that Western science is rooted in a colonial history of violence and oppression. This work has forced us to question the neutrality of science and of knowledge in general. This critique, which expands the work of Foucault in *Power/knowledge* (1980), reminds us that knowledge never exists outside of relations of power. To view this relationship as neutral is to make natural the violence of coercive knowledge. Glissant's understanding of visibility

provides a compelling understanding for why the state uses tools like surveillance and infiltrators to undermine political movements; the ability to
gain visibility is, to them, a tool for social control.

If transparency is required to understand the other in the Western model,
Glissant develops a theory of relation in which opacity is not only respected
but also essential: "Agree not merely to the right to difference but, carrying
this further, agree also to the right to opacity that is not enclosure within
an impenetrable autarchy but subsistence within an irreducible singularity.
Opacities can coexist and converge, weaving fabrics" (Glissant, 1997: 190).
This perspective works to understand that a true, and equal, relation of
opacity needs to be centered on each individual having the right to opacity—
to being able to keep aspects of themselves free from view of others. It is
by accepting people, without full knowledge of them, that true solidarity
and relation of equal power can be developed. Glissant correctly notes that
transparency hides and ignores relations of power, and that the state's use
of visibility serves as a tool of violence. This is the violence described by
the city of San Francisco's programs against the homeless in the previous
chapter.

Since the homeless live, by definition, primarily within the public sphere
of life, it can be assumed that visibility and transparency are essential parts
of their lives, the assumption is that they are not responsible enough as a
product of them lacking the ability to avoid complete transparency by
escaping into the private sphere of life. Even when the state works to hide
them from the public—in homeless shelters, missions, or service agencies—
they are denied opacity as they are constantly monitored and viewed. Part
of the process of disempowering the homeless is to make transparency an
essential part of their nature.

The demand by the homeless for a right to opacity changes that, and
changes the way we conceive and understand public space. For the homeless, the right of opacity also means a right to privacy, security, and acceptance into the political community, which often requires a private existence
to express yourself in the public space politically. For public space, this
means altering our understanding of public space as space open to the
government's watching eye, and also the power to regulate and control. If
the homeless, who are existing in public space, have a right to opacity, it
means that privacy cannot only be a right in private, but that people and
groups carry the right with them wherever they traverse the world.

This is also a means of blurring the distinction that liberal society makes
between public and private. In liberal politics the public is the space of
political expression and the private is a realm of freedom and privacy from
government intervention. The idea that government should not regulate
what happens in a couple's bedroom, for instance, assumes the existence
and presence of a private bedroom. The same logic rarely applies to the

sexual acts in the "public bedroom" (or even the homeless shelter bedroom) that homeless have access to. If the homeless have the same right to opacity in public as the housed have in their private dwelling, we have to reconceive what public space is and how we think about and engage with it.

Lastly, demanding and having a right to opacity allows for individuals and groups to decide when, and in what ways, they become visible forces. The political power of occupying space—be it taking over public parks, government buildings, protesting, etc.—is compelling because it represents an intentional decision by the people to make themselves visible. When a group has the power to decide when, and in what way, they are transparent, it makes the act much more powerful, and undermines the hierarchical system of power relations that are otherwise present when visibility is not a choice, for the viewed, but an imposition by those with power.

Food Not Bombs, homeless activism and resisting revanchist policies

> Over 6,000 hot meals served for free, not one health complaint. Over 450 arrests for serving free food, not one conviction (Food Not Bombs flier, September 1993: McGarry, 2008: 248)

While sources like the Wall Street Journal, Christian Science Monitor, and *San Francisco Chronicle* columnist Debra Saunders supported the Matrix plan, as did many San Francisco voters as evidenced by the ballot success that Frank Jordan enjoyed during his term, the entire political left in San Francisco opposed it. Most notably, Jordan was resisted by Food Not Bombs, the San Francisco Coalition for the Homeless, and Religious Witness, an interfaith alliance that formed to oppose the Matrix plan. While the Coalition for the Homeless and Religious Witness received more positive coverage in the larger San Francisco papers, it is Food Not Bombs that this chapter focuses on, largely due to their more radical politics and the role they played in promoting constant protests and actions in ways that most frustrated the mayor's administration.

By the time Jordan took office, Food Not Bombs had established itself as one of the most important homeless service groups in the city. In August 1993 the group had more than 75 regular members and was serving over 500 meals a day, making them the fourth largest food service organization in San Francisco, all without accepting government funding, having a paid staff, or a fixed office or cooking space. During Jordan's term, the group organized meal services twice a day, once in Civic Center Park and again at UN Plaza; every Monday they also served a meal at Golden Gate Park, making a total of 15 meals a week. In addition to their daily meal services,

5.1 Food Not Bombs cook house in San Francisco 1995

which took them in front of City Hall and into the heart of the financial district, the group shouted down the mayor at his public press conferences, organized a tent-city occupation of UN Plaza during the 50th anniversary of the United Nations, organized massive protests in Golden Gate Park against the expansion of Matrix in 1995, and protested in front of the mayor's home on multiple occasions. During Jordan's four years, more than 700 arrests and citations were handed out to Food Not Bombs activists; Keith McHenry nearly faced life in prison for a third-strikes violation (which would have made McHenry the first white person sent to prison for life under California's "three strikes" law); the group convinced a state judge to overturn the city's injunction against the group's public feedings;[1] and even Amnesty International and the ACLU came to the group's defense. At the end of Jordon's term, the *San Francisco Chronicle* asked every candidate in an early mayoral debate what they would do about Food Not Bombs. Of the five major candidates at the time, only Jordan stated that he would continue to arrest them for distributing food without a permit.

Going back to the early Jordan administration, before the development of the Matrix plan, Food Not Bombs actively opposed the city's homelessness policies—most notably the city's constant arresting and citing of homeless people for public order issues. The group's meal services in busy public spaces gave the public and media the ability to witness police harassment of the homeless, making them more visible. Food Not Bombs never let down its guard after Jordan's election. In fact, Jordan's harsh language against the homeless only motivated the group to become more militant and active. Energized, the group increased its meal service from daily to fifteen times a week. Not only did they expand the number of meals they shared, but also moved to Civic Center Park right in front of City Hall, one of the locations the police were attempting to remove the homeless from.

Early in the Jordan administration, Food Not Bombs activists were not being arrested, in contrast to Agnos, prompting Keith McHenry to tell a reporter, "We don't get arrested for serving free food anymore" (Brazil, 1993). Even though McHenry and Food Not Bombs activists were no longer getting arrested, the administration was not supportive of the group's politics and actions. Early in his administration Jordan asked the court system for another injunction against the group's public feedings in Civic Center Park. As before, the courts complied with the administration's request, making public feedings by the group a misdemeanor (breaking a court injunction) and not a mere citation (distributing food without a permit). And, as before, the group was not deterred: even with a court injunction against them, they served meals daily in Civic Center Park.

The presence of the group in San Francisco politics caused the hostility between City Hall and Food Not Bombs to escalate more quickly with the passage of the Matrix program. Instantly, Food Not Bombs became one of the most active voices against the program. The first organized protest against the plan was on September 16, 1993, two weeks after Jordan implemented the Matrix program. The first protest the group organized was a joint protest and meal service in Civic Center Park. Unlike the previous meal services in Civic Center, the police showed up to arrest the activists for breaking the court injunction and tension quickly escalated, as Food Not Bombs members, and others coming to get free food, pelted the police with bagels as they confiscated the food that the group had brought to serve. During this protest four Food Not Bombs activists were arrested, and shortly following the protest Angela Alioto, the most left-leaning member of the Board of Supervisors, brought forward a proposal to decriminalize Food Not Bombs' feedings, but the proposal was defeated (*San Francisco Chronicle* Reporter, 1993).

The protests against the Matrix program continued as Food Not Bombs, on September 29, brought together hundreds of activists and homeless residents to congregate in and block Civic Center Park. Food Not Bombs, chanting "Food Not Cops," again pelted the police with bagels when they tried to arrest members of the group. Much like the first protest against the Matrix program, the city responded with force, arresting 35 people and

5.2 Eating food on the ground

setting the tone for the remaining year and a half of the Jordan administration. One Food Not Bombs activist, Terry Mullan, explained, "We're just defending our food table and we are not going to make it easy for them to take us away" (Lynch, 1993: A30). In response to Mullan, Police Commander Dennis Martel, the officer in charge of orchestrating the Matrix Plan, replied, "This rally had nothing to do with the homeless. It was a planned demonstration . . . for publicity" (Lynch, 1993: A30). Echoing his predecessor Art Agnos, Frank Jordan asserted, "Keith McHenry is welcome to serve food legally anywhere the law permits. If the intent is to feed the poor by legal means, there are ways to accomplish that goal" (Lynch, 1993: A30). Of course, the accepted space for feeding the homeless was out of the sight of tourists and the financial sector.

From September on, Food Not Bombs and other groups organized large protests almost weekly, and every single meal service—all fifteen every week—became a protest against the city's war against the homeless. Much like the protests that started off their resistance to the Matrix program, nearly every Food Not Bombs meal service attracted a police presence, activists were arrested for providing free food to the homeless. Although people were not arrested every day, there was always an imminent threat of arrest, confiscation of resources (tables, bowls, containers, pamphlets, cars, etc.), or other forms of harassment. It was this daily harassment of the group during the last half of 1993 that prompted Amnesty International in 1994 to contact the mayor's office and threaten to list Food Not Bombs activists as Prisoners of Conscious. Though Amnesty International never initiated an active campaign to support Food Not Bombs activists, their public condemnation of the city's actions gave a major boost to the group's political visibility, and provided support for the group's claim that the city was unfairly harassing them.

In addition to organizing meals multiple times a day, Food Not Bombs began organizing actions to disrupt the mayor's press conferences and discredit his administration at any opportunity that presented itself. Targeting the Matrix plan, members of the group began attending the mayor's public press conferences, shouting down the mayor, carrying protest signs, and, in general, disrupting the events. These actions demonstrated that the Citizen Mayor's actions were not popular amongst the citizens, and that he was unable to establish order, even at his own events. Similarly, the group protested at Jordan's campaign events during his 1995 re-election bid. The group would set up tables in front of campaign dinner spots, for instance, with signs and fliers highlighting the mayor's record on homelessness, housing, and gutting of social services. The group also began protesting in front of the mayor's house on October 10, 1993 (Lynch, 1993; Lehrman, 1995). At the first house demonstration over 200 people gathered to protest the mayor's policies. Twenty-one people were arrested as the group banged drums, jeered the mayor, and made a ruckus. During the protest, some members of the homeless community threatened to turn his front yard into a tent-city, but after the arrests they backed down on that claim and disbanded (Lynch, 1993: A30).

Following the home demonstration, Food Not Bombs member Keith McHenry humorously attempted to remove Frank Jordan's name from the mayor's office door. In the process, the mayor's aide contacted the City Hall police. The police chased McHenry from the mayor's door throughout the entire City Hall, until McHenry barricaded himself inside the office of Board of Supervisors Hallinan's office. The police finally entered through the window in order to detain and arrest McHenry; on the way out of the building he screamed "Police State, Police State" (Levy, 1993). Actions like this, which created chaos in City Hall and public meetings, became a regular part of life for the mayor and for other members of the Board of Supervisors.

The largest action that Food Not Bombs organized was a week-long event to counter the 50th anniversary of the United Nations, which started on June 25, 1995. During the week, Food Not Bombs and other groups organized a tent-city occupation of UN Plaza and a 24-hour soup kitchen, as well as daily protests and street occupations. The protest coincided with a city festival celebrating the 50th anniversary of the signing of the UN Declaration of Human Rights, and highlighting ongoing human rights abuses in San Francisco and the United States more generally. While hundreds of groups protested the UN celebration—with topics ranging from AIDS and war to Tibet and Bosnia, the San Francisco police stated: "The one group that has been causing the most trouble this weekend is Food Not Bombs and, in my opinion, they would be the likeliest source of a problem" (Delgado, Winokur, & Allison, 1995).

In anticipation of the protest, Food Not Bombs put out a call to action, and expanded the protest to a national Food Not Bombs gathering. Activists from nearly 40 chapters of Food Not Bombs—from Seattle to San Diego and Berkeley to Boston—came to provide support. This reinforcement to the already large activist-base of Food Not Bombs allowed the group to maintain the soup kitchen and tent-city even with daily police arrests and confiscations. In the first two nights alone, 61 Food Not Bombs activists were arrested for blocking an intersection and resisting arrest, 9 more for distributing food without a permit, and 12 more in a concurrent action at the Presidio. Overall, the police and Food Not Bombs played a weekend-long cat-and-mouse game, in which "day after day, in violation of city health ordinances, the activists smuggled bagels, soup, and fruit into the plaza to feed the city's homeless. And day after day, the cops tried to prevent the food distribution, arresting numerous people in the process" (Delgado, Winokur, & Allison, 1995). By the end of the weekend-long action, the police appeared frustrated with arresting Food Not Bombs activists. Police Sergeant Rene Laprevotte told the *San Francisco Chronicle*, "We've been about 75 percent successful in intercepting the food before it's distributed. But to me it's just not worth the hassle. If they just let [Food Not Bombs] distribute their stuff, nine out of ten people wouldn't eat it. It's really crummy food" (Delgado, Winokur, & Allison, 1995). This was not the first time that police officers mentioned frustration at carrying out the mayor's orders. For instance, one anonymous police officer told the *San Francisco Chronicle*:

> Citing these people is not a normal thing. It's done, but is not a regular part of our duties. But we are gearing up for UN50 and we are specifically being told to do it now . . . A lot of us don't like going out citing somebody for being within 500 feet of a stupid off-ramp, but if you're told to do it, you do it. I think we all would rather not be involved in Matrix. We think it is a political thing, and we would rather not get involved in somebody's political career. (Johnson, 1995)

However, the majority of police officers were interested in maintaining order during the UN50 protests. Lt. Larry Barsetti, one of the officers in charge of maintaining order during the protest, stated, "If we had a plane, we'd use it, too. We're looking for anything that would disrupt civil order" (Delgado, Winokur, & Allison, 1995).

5.3 Arrests at UN Plaza: riot police confronting Food Not Bombs at UN protests, 1998

A few months after the UN50 protests, in August 1995, Food Not Bombs worked with others to coordinate a series of large homeless protests in Golden Gate Park. The August 28 protest in the park was a sleep in, in which homeless residents and political activists laid down in the park after nightfall and, flaunting the law, camped in the open en masse. These protests occurred shortly following the mayor's renewed call for Golden Gate Park residents to be evicted. The massive scale of the protests kept the police from sweeping the park for two days. After being evicted from Golden Gate Park, homeless residents and Food Not Bombs activists organized and protested in front of the mayor's house. Egg Allen, one of the homeless protestors speaking out against the mayor's plan asked, "Why is it that he wants people living in Golden Gate Park to move back onto the streets? With the cuts he is making [in services], people won't even be able to sleep in doorways" (Lehrman, 1995). The mayor did not go out and talk to the protestors, who at that point had become a daily part of his reality. Instead he told the press, "They're saying the people have every right to camp anywhere they want, to take over our parks. It's something I won't allow" (Hatfield, Glover et al., 1995). Once again, the discourse out of the mayor's office was about viewing the homeless as invaders of the city, and viewing him and his administration as the group protecting the city.

In short, from 1993 onward Food Not Bombs was a gadfly for the mayor's office. The group remained constantly in the public eye and forced the mayor to publicly address issues of homelessness, even when he did not want to. They refused to back down or weaken their protest, even after receiving over 700 citations and arrests. Though the administration prided themselves on protecting public order, the city was never able to keep Food Not Bombs in check, as the group never missed a meal service, never missed a protest, and never missed an opportunity to confront the mayor. By the end of Jordan's four-year term, Food Not Bombs had become something of a cause célèbre with thousands of active supporters in the Bay Area, including the punk band Green Day, which played a benefit concert to help cover Food Not Bombs' legal fees. Internationally, the press from San Francisco helped expand and galvanize the overall Food Not Bombs movement as the group expanded from 40 chapters in 1992 to nearly 100, including chapters throughout Western Europe and South America, by 1995 (Crass, 1995). In effect, Food Not Bombs provided a constant public check on the mayor's anti-homeless politics. They also resisted the mayor's attempts to make the homeless either publically invisible or politically marginalized. By regularly coordinating protests, Food Not Bombs kept the homeless in public view, empowered the homeless residents to make demands of the city—effectively making them political subjects—and forced the issue of homelessness into the public debate. Their ability to undermine his administration's enforcement of anti-homeless provisions, and their ability to publically harass him, partially led to Frank Jordan losing his re-election bid.

In the concluding section of this chapter, we explore the theoretical implication of the Matrix program by focusing on two primary theoretical issues: first, the impact of the anti-citizen frame the Jordan administration made on the homeless and, secondly, the impact of increased surveillance and top-down visibility on the homeless community. Both these issues are theoretically important for the twenty-first century, as neoliberal homelessness politics has permeated nearly every major urban center and, as Craig Willse (2015) has argued, a system of managing the homeless has emerged that has dovetailed with the needs for economic neoliberalism and a racialized system of benefits and privileges that marks the white supremacists' political regime of the United States.

Food Not Bombs forced a continual discussion about homelessness, often on their terms, making homelessness the front and center in San Francisco politics, by framing the issue as "Why is the mayor arresting people for feeding the homeless?" Food Not Bombs highlighted the revanchist policies of Jordan, in a city named after Saint Francis and known for its compassion and tolerance. Food Not Bombs' ability to frame Matrix and homelessness in San Francisco highlighted the mayor's inability to control much of anything.

Conclusion

The homeless community resisted Jordan's attempts to sanitize the city of their presence, and with the help of Food Not Bombs they worked to forge their own space within the city and reclaim the commons back from commercial interests. But, bringing back in Glissant, their act of making themselves visible differs drastically from the actions of the state, which tried to make them visible to the state but hidden from the consumer public. Fundamentally, the difference between the state and the activist group's understanding of visibility has to do with intent and agency. By making themselves politically visible, in strategic ways, Food Not Bombs was able to undermine the state's attempts to regulate and define public space. In doing so, they showed that the decision to be visible can, in many cases, undermine hierarchies of power and, in this case, they weakened the state's ability to regulate and monitor the homeless community fully—thus also providing the homeless with more of a right of opacity than they would otherwise have.

The controlling and claiming of public space was also important to Food Not Bombs' success in undermining the Jordan administration's attempts to regulate and control space. During the Jordan years, Food Not Bombs fought a daily battle to maintain the ability to distribute food in public space, a fight that was most conflictual in the high-profile Civic Center and UN Plaza. From September 1993, when Matrix was first expanded, to December 1995, the city regularly arrested and harassed Food Not Bombs activists for distributing food. The goal was to remove their presence, and the homeless residents they attracted, from these public spaces. Even so, the group never missed a meal service and was always present in the Civic Center and UN Plaza. The group served as a constant nuisance to city officials and showed the city's limitation in forging political order.

The group's occupation of UN Plaza during the important UN50 events demonstrated its ability to take over and control space, even in the face of intense police presence. This week-long occupation, late in Jordan's term, served as his "Camp Agnos," illustrating his inability to maintain public order and to regulate and control public space. While Food Not Bombs' reclaiming of public space was only temporary in this instance, it was a reminder to the mayor and the city at large that no one has a monopoly over public space.

Food Not Bombs attempted to shatter the division between public and private. Reclaiming the commons was not just about creating a common space for all to enjoy, but about making common space a communal space, a space for the development of politics, friendships, and the living of lives. By making public space a location where meals are eaten, assemblies held, and bonds created, the division between public and private is also weakened. Since liberalism regularly uses the public/private divide as a way to separate and exclude, the queering or shattering of that border is a radical act that opens up the possibility for what Rancière calls *politics*. This shattering of the consensus of the *police* is a means to open up space for a transformation of the politics in the city.

In Bernardo Bertolucci's 2003 movie *The Dreamers*, there is a scene that examines the lives of one American and two French students, as their lives slip toward depression and suicide during the Paris uprising in 1968. In the end their lives are saved when someone throws a rock through their window, bringing them into the public uprising that was happening just outside their apartment. The rock shattered the division between public and private and brought them out into the streets (Bertolucci, 2003).

Turning the broken-window metaphor on its head, *The Dreamers* shows that "breaking the spell," as black bloc protestors call the shattering of windows during protests, also breaks open the isolating boundaries of atomized private life, exposing an exciting world on the other side. In the film narrative, the broken window does not show the degeneration of the social body, but is an expression of a radical desire to shatter the old bonds of society and forge new ones. This is the anarchist version of broken-windows theorizing: the power of the people to rise and smash the boundaries that keep them imprisoned. When the window is smashed the personal becomes political, the private becomes public, the hidden becomes visible, and the excluded depoliticized express their power.

Notes

1   It was ruled that the city was unfairly enforcing the ban on serving food in public because they were not doing the same to other organizations or individuals. For instance, Mayor Frank Jordan in 1995 had a campaign event "Franks with Frank" in which he gave out free hot dogs to his supporters. Much like Food Not Bombs, Jordan never got a permit to serve the food, yet he was not cited or arrested for breaking the ban.

6

Bolt cutters and the politics of expropriation: Homes Not Jails, urban squatting, and gentrification

I wake up in a cold room in the south side of Chicago: while the house is in great shape for a squat, the windows are drafty and the cold air seeps into the room. If you have ever been in a Chicago cold, you know that no number of layers of clothes and no number of blankets can keep you completely warm. The cold in the city is the kind that gets into your bones, making them ache. But the pain is not all horrible; the pinch of the cold lets you know you are alive, and makes it easier to hop out of bed and get started with your day.

In this instance, the getting up and moving was essential. Some friends and I had traveled to Chicago for a series of protests at and around May Day, titled "Carnivals against Capitalism." The protests, which were filled with activists, clowns, circus performers, drummers, and puppets, were a celebration of the power of play and resistance during the heart of oppressive George W. Bush presidency. Before getting ready for the protest, my friends and I ran down the creaky stairs from our attic rooms and towards the wafting smell of freshly brewed coffee and the underwhelming feel of dumpstered bagels in your mouth.

This squat, one of the few I have ever stayed in for any period of time, had been around for years, and was one of many in the neighborhood. A product of the racialized poverty of Chicago's south side, these old, large houses had run into disrepair, as city money and private equity, segregation and city policy, white flight and white disinterest depressed the local housing market. Many years after I had spent the week in that squat, the area was facing a supposed resurgence, as the city tore down and sold the housing projects in the area to local developers who not only turned the former public housing into lofts for middle-class professionals, but also started buying and renovating, or demolishing, these old homes to make way for fancy new houses and artisan businesses. Soon the neighborhood was up and coming, hip, and fun, all of which are just code words for white and middle-class. And the old residents? They were mostly pushed east, past the border with Indiana and into East Chicago, Hammond, and Gary Indiana. Poverty gets concentrated even further and the city increasingly becomes a playground for the rich. And the poor? They are not just evicted from their homes; they are kicked out of their state!

The chapters up to now have focused on Food Not Bombs, and the public feedings and protests they orchestrated in San Francisco. This chapter shifts focus on Frank Jordan and the city's response to Homes Not Jails, a sister group of Food Not Bombs, which opens up unused apartments and houses for the homeless to occupy.

This chapter shows that Jordan, who waged an all-out war against the homeless and Food Not Bombs, had a much more nuanced response to Homes Not Jails. The squatting rights group was not uniformly attacked at all instances, but the group, which was illegally housing up to 500 residents on a single night, was treated differently depending on the public nature of their actions. When the group held public occupations—forcing the private back into the public—the city responded aggressively and harshly towards the activists. When they acted mostly in the cover of night, on the other hand, moving the homeless into unused rooms in abandoned houses, the city tended to turn a blind eye. This chapter seeks to understand why, and disentangle the politics of squatting, placing it in a dialogue with the role that public and private space play in homeless resistance and anti-homeless city politics.

This chapter begins with a brief discussion of the process of gentrification, and the role of neoliberalism in housing, followed by an overview of the main concepts found in academic work on squatting. Lastly, it looks at the history of San Francisco's Homes Not Jails, including a short list of the group's actions, as well as a discussion of the relationship between squatting and struggles for urban space.

Gentrification and the housing crisis

Gentrification has started to feel like a natural part of city life. In cities around the country, urban centers, which had been severely impacted by suburbanization and white flight during the 1960s–1990s, began to receive huge influxes of private and public money. The result of this flow of money was redevelopment, and, as is almost always the case, where the money flows, the white and middle-class in the United States tend to follow.

In a conversation with my friend Joel Olson, at a conference hotel bar, we jokingly discussed the cycle of modern urban gentrification. It starts with squats, infoshops, and punks, who will live anywhere they can get away with. To many anarchists the authenticity of living and having an infoshop in a historically non-white and working class neighborhood also makes it a more radical act. Before long, the numbers of white punks make the area seem edgy, cool, and unique enough for artists and the white queer community to move in. The neighborhood now starts to become hip and edgy—a place with independent coffee shops, used book stores, great ethnic restaurants, and pockets of its old non-white working-class character. As the racial and class make-up starts to change, it quickly becomes the hot spot for wealthy suburban transplants and upper middle-class professionals. The original residents have now all relocated; the pockets of their non-white working-class community have been turned into boutiques and hip chains. The infoshops, squats, and punks have all been evicted. The artists and queer community? They have both seen rents raised beyond what they can pay and have grown bored of the sterile new feel, moving on to the next up-and-coming part of town. Like most silly joke conversations, ours centered on hyperbole, but, at the same time, pinpointed a reality that we both saw: that gentrification goes through different cycles, even if the structure of those cycles might look different in different places.

This is the current cycle of gentrification. Capital is constantly looking towards new and upcoming neighborhoods, searching for places in which housing values have plummeted, and where easy renovations can revitalize a neighborhood and maximize the wealth they can squeeze out of a community. The formerly gentrified areas will slowly become no longer the it-places, and housing prices might even decrease over time, to the point in which the developers will once again gentrify the neighborhood. With that we see the circle of neoliberal capitalist life; it is an image of a snake eating its own tail, a narrative of never ending removal and relocation for the poor, a constant funneling of wealth—both public and private—towards the economic elite.

The process of gentrification needs to be understood not as a natural product of capitalist cycles—though it is tied to cycles of urban capitalism—but as an intentionally developed system. Gentrification is the direct result of public policy and private equity, and represents a state–capital partnership. This process has become so central to urban life in the United States because the conditions of neoliberalism have required increasing public–private economic partnerships, and have led to cities corporatizing and sanitizing their public space due to the drastic decrease in federal support for urban locals. Gentrification becomes a means for cities to increase the funding of their coffers, to increase their public image, and to attract a larger tourist base. As such, cities around the nation have turned to policies that promote this outcome by criminalizing the homeless, privatizing public buildings and public space, using taxpayer money to build sports stadiums and convention centers, and to either relocate or remove public housing and services for low-income residents. In taking advantage of extreme poverty and need, the developers pit class, racial, and generational groups against each other. The blame is easily directed at the newest residents, but the developers, most of whom the residents will never see or even know the name of, get to laugh all the way to the bank.

This is part of what Craig Willse sees as the managing of poverty, housing, and life in the neoliberal city. In his work he argues that the distribution and cost of housing, which is largely influenced by policy, is part of a bio- and necropolitics of urban existence. Through government policy we decide who has access to housing and who is primarily excluded from it. As Willse writes:

> To be without a house, to be homeless, is not only to be not-housed, to be in nothing, outside housing. Quite the opposite. It is to be very much caught inside this monster that distributed life chances and death likelihoods. To live within this system in which everyone is caught, including those of us who are housed. To live without a house, or without the guarantee of continued access to a house, is to be made especially vulnerable in this system of housing, to be exposed to the worst of its violence. This violent exposure is a condition we can describes as "housing insecurity." To live subject to housing insecurity is also to endure the making insecure of health and life that accompanies a lack of safe and stable housing. (Willse, 2015: 2)

To put this clearly: access to, and exclusion from, housing is part of a broader system that is constructed, maintained, and defined by government policy and the structuring of the economy.

The role and influence of policy on access to home ownership works to undermine the liberal understanding of public and private, and the entire neoliberal analysis of homelessness—which individualizes the causes of homelessness and blames the homeless for their situation. By denaturalizing the housing market and situating it within a broader policy-social nexus, it also reframes houselessness as an intentional government program—one that, when you combine the money and efforts at managing homelessness, helps recirculate money and, just like gentrification, filter it to certain people and industries.

One of the primary anarchist ways to interrupt the capitalist housing cycle is squatting. At its theoretical core, squatting attempts to undermine the logic of private ownership by providing a means for activists to expropriate dwellings for social good. The next section explores the academic work on squatting, to situate the experience of Homes Not Jails within the broader work on squatting.

Direct action and the expropriation of dwellings: background theory on squatting

For them to say that we steal their unused property, while they speculate on the rental market, is criminal. They steal when they charge us rent, as opposed to us stealing when we squat. We should not ask whether it is a crime to "steal" a piece of property, but whether it's a crime to charge rent. (Jeremy Graham, Homes Not Jails activist; Corr, 1999: 26)

For those who face extreme poverty, it is often necessary to commit numerous illegal acts on a daily basis, just to survive. Nik Heynen and Don Mitchell refer to these acts as part of a geography of survival[1] (Heynen 2010; Mitchell and Heynen, 2009). The geography of survival includes not only panhandling and urban camping, but also the distribution of government services and the process of squatting. While squatting exists in nearly every location imaginable, and is a common way for the homeless and radical activists to acquire housing, the topic has received scant academic discussion for the way it operates as a political tactic. This does not mean that squatting has not been used regularly as part of the repertoire of action for the housing rights and poor people's movements. As an example, the Association for Community Organizations for Reform Now, or ACORN, in 1985 squatted 25 buildings in Brooklyn with relative success, as the city handed over 58 abandoned buildings to ACORN and Mutual Housing Association to run as low-income housing.[2] However, the city handed over the buildings on the condition that ACORN would refrain from using squatting as a tactic in the future (Pruijt, 2003: 141). The use of squatting as a tactic tends to make it a relatively short-lived and public approach, designed to elicit government reaction and provide space for organizations to compromise and make gains.

The squatters' movement, on the other hand, views squatting as an end in and of itself. The goal of the squatters' movement is to create a culture and community around squatting. In this regard,

> squatting itself is at the centre. It is a community of squatters who cooperate when new buildings are squatted and in the defense against evictions. Organization is bottom-up and network structured. There is little formal organization; informal leadership exists, however . . . There is a do-it-yourself ethic and an ideology of self-determination. (Pruijt, 2003: 143)

In effect, squatters' movements tend to embrace a form of radical politics that George Katsiaficas refers to as autonomous politics. Katsiaficas, in *The subversion of politics*, examines the European autonomous movement—consisting of radical leftists who are autonomous of political parties, unions, and the state—which used squatting as one of their central political acts. In Katsiaficas' narrative of German, Dutch, and Italian autonomous movements, the squats played a radicalizing role in the community. Living in the squats radicalized the youth through everyday experiences with direct democracy, direct action, and constant police struggles. In effect, "living behind barricades became a way of life for many squatters, the illegality of their everyday lives radicalized their attitude towards the state and hardened their own feelings of self-importance" (Katsiaficas, 1997: 91).[3] Overall this movement consisted of mostly radical middle-class youth, artists, and punks, who embraced a radical anti-capitalist politics, centered on a do-it-yourself philosophy.[4] According to Richard Day, in *Gramsci is dead*, squatters' movements should not be viewed as drop-out movements looking to remove themselves from society. Squatting is often a way to free up one's time to engage in other forms of political action and activism, since the squatters no longer need to work to pay rent (Day, R. J. F., 2005: 21).

According to Pruijt, squatters' movements, unlike housing movements, are difficult for government agencies to co-opt or institutionalize. This is because squatters' movements are interested in forming a non-capitalist housing arrangement and therefore squat largely due to a political conviction. To highlight the difference, Pruijt compares the early 1980s' New York housing movement, typified by ACORN, with the late 1980s' Lower East Side squatter movement. In his analysis, ACORN welcomed the opportunity to negotiate with the city and turn squatted houses into non-profit administered affordable housing, while the Lower East Side squatters refused to negotiate with the city, organized mass demonstrations in support of homeless residents in Tompkins Square, and harassed and vandalized gentrifying efforts in the neighborhood. Even without negotiation, the squatters gained legal access to some of their squats. For instance, ABC No Rio, a squatted social center, was sold to an artist collective for $1 on the condition that the group raise the $200,000 needed to renovate and bring the building up to code. Though the building was sold, government officials never directly negotiated with squatters, but with the artist collective that used the space as a gallery.

In addition, anarchist and other radical theorists have generally argued that squatting is a radical act, as it "undermines the singular meaning of home that has come to dominate the American landscape" (Roy, 2003: 482) by questioning the legitimacy of private property and undermining the landlord–tenant relationship. Housing issues have been central to anarchist activism. According to Peter Kropotkin, the classical anarchist prince, the root of capitalist exploitation was not surplus value, as Marx stated, but poverty. To Kropotkin, people sell their labor for a starvation wage only because they need the money in order to survive. Expressing this, Kropotkin writes:

> Everywhere you will find that the wealth of the wealthy springs from the poverty of the poor. This is why an anarchist society need not fear the advent of a Rothschild who would settle in its midst. If every member of the community knows that after a few hours of productive toil he will have a right to all the pleasures that civilization procures . . . he will not sell his strength for a starvation wage. No one will volunteer to work for the enrichment of your Rothschild. His gold guineas will be only so many pieces of metal—useful for various purposes, but incapable of breeding more. (Kropotkin, 1975: 231)

In other words, Kropotkin claims that if goods and services were distributed to everyone based on need, no one would sell their labor. To equalize and democratize distribution, anarchists have tried to confront capitalism and the state by creating alternative institutions. Food Not Bombs and Homes Not Jails squarely fit within this counter-institutional framework.

The creation of egalitarian distribution based on need is central to Kropotkin's understanding of revolutionary action. For instance, in *The conquest of bread*, Kropotkin discusses the need to organize and distribute, through non-state and non-market mechanisms, goods and services for all to use. He contends that a revolutionary movement will be successful only if it is able to distribute fairly, efficiently, and communally. Kropotkin provides possible examples of how the masses could collectively expropriate food, clothing, and shelter in such a way that hunger and other deprivations do not force the masses back into the exploiting arms of the counter-revolutionaries. While food is essential, it is the expropriation of housing that "contains in germ the social revolution" (Kropotkin, 1975: 240). This is because housing and property, unlike food or clothing, is fundamental to the construction and maintenance of a capitalist society. In other words, the expropriation of housing undermines the foundation of liberal society—the sanctity of private property. In Kropotkin's account of expropriation of dwellings, a community collectively takes inventory of housing, has a direct assembly to discuss housing, and then starts placing people within houses. Thus a single person with a three-bedroom house would either move to a one-bedroom flat or have two roommates put within the house. Likewise, a family of seven stuffed into a two-bedroom flat would be given a place with more rooms.

Building on Kropotkin's idea is Colin Ward's work on anarchist housing and urban planning. Central to his work is the role of squatters, land occupiers, and tenant rights movements, who highlight the fact that the masses can—democratically and justly—construct, distribute, and organize their own lives. To Ward, anarchist institutions distribute goods fairly and efficiently, since they are fluid, dynamic, and directly connected to the will and desires of the community. This process is a threat to state bureaucrats, who argue that they are needed to ensure that goods are distributed fairly, and are equally a threat to free-marketers, who claim that only the market can distribute goods fairly (Ward, 1973). In *Housing: an anarchist perspective*, Ward contends, "The real triumph of the squatters' movement, is that it has called the bluff of those who believe in political action. The squatters have shown that they can rehabilitate housing more quickly and more effectively than the official system can" (Ward, 1976: 34). Katsiaficas promotes a similar view of squatting, arguing that the squatters' movement, in Germany especially, allowed the creation of a radical autonomous political movement. This movement confronted racism and classism, and worked to undermine German middle-class understandings of life and politics as being safe, stable, and under control (Katsiaficas, 1997).

Countering this anarchist stance on squatting, Ananya Roy provides, in "Paradigms of Propertied Citizenship: Transnational Techniques of Analysis," a few warnings for squatters. First, she warns the group from fetishizing self-help, which she claims has been used to justify government inaction in poor communities, as governments increasingly look to poor communities to lift themselves up from the bootstraps. In addition, self-help creates a form of voluntarist citizenship that justifies the squatters' actions because of the improvement they provide to the property. As she puts it:

> In an era of liberalization, the ideology of sweat equity shifts the burden of coping from the state to the poor, putting into place a 'voluntarist' citizenship. As homelessness policies have been dominated by the trope of the undeserving poor, so recent Third World debates have coalesced around the hope of a self-sufficient informal sector capable of Herculean efforts. These are extreme positions on the same discursive continuum of morality and behaviorism, both serving to legitimate state withdrawal from social commitments. (Roy, 2003: 481)

In effect, Roy warns against claiming that sweat equity and the work of the poor can solve the housing problem. Doing so, in her argument, only provides further justification for the state to withdraw from this the housing dilemma.

Second, Roy contends that

> . . . although the doctrine of adverse possession bears the promise of legalizing squatting, of formalizing informality, it requires the 'open and notorious use' of property. And yet when squats are open and notorious, they are often quickly ended through evictions . . . The doctrine requires a process that is impossible to uphold. (Roy, 2003: 481)

Thus she warns that squatting, to be effective, runs the risk of getting stuck in a cycle of evictions and exploitation that has plagued much of the Third World squatting movements. Her warning is that the labor and sweat of the squatters will be taken and used by the land owners and developers through a process in which squatters build and develop a neighborhood or house, which they are then forcibly evicted from, and their labor is stolen by absentee landlords who have their land improved at no cost to them.

The complex nature of squatting and its relationship to neoliberal urban housing economies is complicated, and there is no clear black-and-white position that can be taken. Is squatting a threat to the liberal homeownership system? Or does it serve as a way for urban developers to cheaply begin the process of redeveloping a community? The answer, as shown below, for Homes Not Jails in San Francisco, is yes. Yes to both. Squatting in San Francisco functioned, at times, as a threat to the Jordan administration, and other times it was a welcomed act.

All you need is a bolt cutter: Homes Not Jails and the politics of squatting in San Francisco

We teach people how to use a crowbar to pop open a door, how to get in different kinds of windows, how to use a bread knife to flip the lock latch on a window, how to re-key locks. The number of people who have learned the skills has to be in the hundreds, if not over a thousand people. (Jeremy Graham, Homes Not Jails activist; Corr, 1999: 25)

In the mid-1990s, San Francisco had an estimated 6,500 unused houses or apartments—enough to house the entire homeless population of the city (Steinberg, 1994). With so many unused rooms and houses, Homes Not Jails became the first formal squatting organized in the city. The group was formed in November 1992, following a film showing that was sponsored by Food Not Bombs. During the movie, which detailed a squatting campaign in Philadelphia, Keith McHenry from Food Not Bombs and Ted Gullickson from the San Francisco Tenants Union, an organization that provides practical and legal advice for renters, decided to take action. Their plan was to open up an abandoned homeless shelter at 90 Golden Gate, whose owner was intentionally keeping the building empty. After the film showing, the 30 other people in attendance joined McHenry and Gullickson, and the first Homes Not Jails meeting and squat started. That first squat housed five homeless residents for nearly two months, until the residents were evicted on January 3, 1993 (Corr, 1999: 23). Homes Not Jails engages in two types of actions: covert squatting and public occupations

Homes Not Jails and the politics around covert squatting

The covert squats are "meant to assert propertied rights for the homeless, specifically through the doctrine of 'adverse possession,' which recognizes the 'highest and best use of property' and under stringent conditions makes possible the legalization of squatting" (Roy, 2003: 480). Under adverse possession, squatters need to show that they have openly and intentionally been squatting a building for at least five years, pay back taxes owed on that property, and show proof that they have improved the building. If the building was not occupied, even for one night, or if a judge feels that the squatters had not been ideal neighbors, then the adverse possession claim is lost. As of today, Homes Not Jails has been unable to take over any building titles through adverse possession, though they came very close in 1999, when they paid the back rent on a squat on Page Street that squatters had been occupying for six years (Wilson, 1999). In the end, the judge ruled against the group's claim.

In creating their covert squats, Homes Not Jails begins by scouting an area, looking for vacant houses, and then researching who owns the building and whether any plans are in place to renovate or demolish the building. The group compiles a list of squatable buildings and then, at least once a week, members of the group go around the city and break into houses. When they break in, the group looks for signs of people living there or work being done on the building—from mail or newspapers to paint or trash. If a building seems to be vacant, the activists do some clean-up, change the locks, and wait a week to see if anyone has noticed their presence. If everything checks out they move homeless residents into the building.

All Homes Not Jails squats have three rules: first, there will be no violence against other residents of the squat, or against the police when they evict; second, there will be no alcohol or drug use within the squat; and third, all squats will be run using a consensus form of decision making, and all residents must be involved in the process. In addition, each squat runs on a principle of sweat equity. Sweat equity means that:

In lieu of rent, HNJ expects all squatters to clean, paint, and even make structural improvements to their squats, both covert and public . . . [T]hrough sweat equity, homeless people live more comfortably, improve housing values, exchange construction skills, and emphasize the responsibility attended to any right to housing. Sweat equity works well for the many homeless people who are skilled workers but are unemployed, unfairly evicted, or victim to some other structural inequity. For the significant proportion of homeless people who struggle with substance abuse or mental illness, sweat equity offers additional benefits. 'Sweat equity' gives people the opportunity to participate in a common project and create an extended family in which homeless people have a place to heal. (Corr, 1999: 21)

Sweat equity, which has a long history as it was used by frontier homesteaders, is currently used by Habitat for Humanity, and is common in squatting villages in the Third World (Roy, 2003).

One expression of Homes Not Jails' policy of sweat equity appears in a draft proposal to the city in 1998, when they nearly gained legal title for the property at 3250 17th Street, an unused house that was owned by the federal government. Under the Homes Not Jails plan, residents of the building would pay 30% of their income, rather than a set amount, for rent and then work on the house for five hours a week on average. In exchange for the sweat equity, residents would gain 1% of the estimated value of the house per year, which would be given to them in a lump sum when they left the house (Corr, 1999: 23). Thus, if I were to live in one of their low-income housing cooperatives making $356 a month from GA, I would pay $107 a month in rent and work on the house for five hours a week. If I lived at the house, valued at $300,000, for two years, when I left to live on my own I would have $6,000 saved up as a nest egg. Under this plan, the formerly homeless resident would live at a rate significantly lower than the city's SRO hotels, create a community, actively gain skills, improve the city's housing infrastructure, and build savings. The group never implemented this plan, however, since it depended on their gaining legal title to a building.

Overall, Homes Not Jails has opened up hundreds of covert squats throughout San Francisco. On average from 1992 through 1997, Homes Not Jails sent scouting groups each week, opening up somewhere between 700 and 800 buildings in total. According to Andres Carr, at their peak, Homes Not Jails was housing up to 500 people a night in their squats. While most of the covert squats lasted less than a month, a handful lasted entire years. For instance, one squat at 850 Hayes Street lasted for two years. The group was nearly successful at gaining legal title on the building until it mysteriously burned down, after the landowner failed to evict the squatters. Another building, which was successfully squatted from 1994 to 1999, was nearly awarded to the group, after they had successfully paid the property's $5,000 back taxes and formed a legal non-profit to administer the building (Wilson, 1999). The city government, then headed by mayor Willie Brown, fought the group and ended up selling the property and giving the money to the former homeowner's sister.

Overall, the group's covert squats received little attention from the police. This does not mean that members of the group were not arrested for squatting. During a five-year period three activists were arrested for trespassing and breaking and entering. According to Homes Not Jails activist Jeremy Graham, at one squat the police came up to the squatters and said, "We have to see somebody leave. Then we don't care what happens. If we get another call later on, we are not necessarily going to come back" (Corr, 1999: 26–27). In another instance, Graham recounts how the cops informed the squatters; "We won't act unless we get complaints from the property owners. We are not really going to try and prosecute people for trying to house themselves" (Corr, 1999: 26). This attitude stands in stark contrast with the attitude of the police towards Food Not Bombs, whose members were being regularly arrested for providing free food in public spaces. This once again highlights the discrepancy between sanctions over private and public actions.

Though the police generally took a lax approach to the group this does not mean that the police and the city endorsed, or even supported, the actions of Homes Not Jails. For instance, shortly following the publicized eviction of the first Homes Not Jails squat, mayor Jordan stated:

> We just cannot allow people to walk into any vacant building and just take it over as a homeless encampment. These are private buildings . . . and if the [owners] ask us to remove people, we try to do so. There are health hazards involved here. There are public safety issues if someone comes into a building and starts a fire. (Quoted in Corr, 1999: 27)

The mayor's comments do two things. First, they reveal his administration's disdain for squatters, claiming that they are illegally occupying a house, depriving someone else of their property and turning it into a housing encampment. Following from this, he reiterates his general stance on the homeless that they are mentally ill and drug addicted, and therefore poses a threat to start a fire or engage in other anti-social behaviors. Second, and more important, Jordan claims that squatting is a civil and private matter between the squatters and the landowners, and not a criminal issue. This stance differs drastically from his stance against Food Not Bombs, for which he organized a police campaign to stop.

Homes Not Jails and the public occupations of building

Jordan's response to public occupations was different. The public squats are meant to garner media attention to their cause, and to highlight that, even in San Francisco, there are vacant houses that could be used to house homeless residents. These public occupations brought attention to the large number of unoccupied houses in the city, put pressure on the city government to enforce housing rights laws, and condemn both slumlords and landlords who intentionally kept houses empty for speculative financial reasons.

Homes Not Jails organized its first public action on Thanksgiving Day, 1992, in which members of Homes Not Jails occupied a vacant property at 250 Taylor Street, owned by Robert Imhoff, a well-known developer in the city. In addition, the house was across the street from Glide Memorial Church, the location of the largest Thanksgiving homeless feed in the city. Homes Not Jails knew that the media would attend Thanksgiving dinner, and realized that by occupying the building across the street, the group could get valuable media attention at no cost. That first public occupation, which culminated in four arrests, brought significant media attention to the lack of affordable housing in San Francisco.

The group planned a public occupation every Thanksgiving and Christmas Day:

> By having actions on Thanksgiving and Christmas, we hope to change the way people view the homeless. The image of homeless people one sees in the media on almost every other day is of people who deserve what they get, people who have only themselves to blame, people who are dirty, don't take care of themselves, and use drugs. You can't give them money because they'll just waste it all. On Thanksgiving and Christmas, you see families and the deserving poor, pathetic, helpless, passive, and grateful for their bowl of soup . . . What we've tried to project is an image of people denied the resources needed to take care of themselves. People who are angry, competent, capable, and, if necessary, people willing to take extreme actions and be arrested and go to jail, if need be. (Quoted in Corr, 1999: 28)

From 1992 to 1998 the group organized a total of 26 public takeovers. At these events 242 people were arrested, with most (nearly 200) being arrested during an occupation of the military housing in the Presidio in protest of city plans to demolish the housing in 1997 (Corr, 1999). Most Homes Not Jails activists had their charges dropped, but the city did spend $100,000 attempting to convict four activists for trespassing and breaking and entering after the Thanksgiving 1993 action.[5] Ultimately, even those activists had their charges dropped.

These public occupations served an important role for the group—garnering media attention and positioning themselves as an important part of the housing movement in the city. For instance, in 1995, Homes Not Jails teamed up with Board of Supervisors member Angela Alioto to draft an affordable housing bill, which would have given the city the power to take unrented buildings to house the homeless, made adverse possession easier to attain, and increased protections for squatters. The bill never passed the Board of Supervisors, but showed the close ties that the group developed with established members of city government, something that Food Not Bombs never achieved.[6]

The group also sought out government owned buildings. Most importantly, the they looked for federally owned property, applying pressure to both city and federal agencies to follow article V of the Stewart B. McKinney Homeless Assistance Act (1987), which stated that "all surplus, excess, under-utilized, and unutilized" federal property be used to house the homeless. The law was designed to force the federal government to use its vacant and unused buildings for housing the homeless but rarely, if ever, does the government do so. Homes Not Jails thought that occupying federally owned buildings would put pressure on the government to do so, or at least that it would force the courts to make a ruling on the law.

The problem for Homes Not Jails was finding unused government owned buildings in San Francisco. The first federally owned squat the group acquired was on Presidents Day in 1993. The group squatted a building at 1211 Polk Street that was seized by the federal government after the house was raided for tax fraud, methamphetamine production, and child pornography, and was then left vacant for four years. Early on in the occupation the group organized a meeting with a federal marshal, who was intrigued by the group's claim, and held off the city eviction of the squatters until he could get the matter settled with his superiors. After much negotiation, the federal government agreed to sell the building to the city of San Francisco for $77,000, well below market price, if the city would use it as a half-way house for at risk-youth. All mayor Jordan had to do was sign a letter of intent and the process would have begun, but he refused to do so, and instead arrested the squatters. Homes Not Jails attempted to re-squat the building two more times over the year, both times being evicted quickly by the police. Finally the building was sold at auction, for over $300,000, to a developer who quickly resold the building for nearly $350,000.[7]

The group also targeted land owned by the California Transit Authority, since California law SB-120 (1993) "authorized Caltrans to lease airspace or other property acquired for highway purposes in San Francisco to a public agency for purpose of an emergency shelter or feeding program for $1 a month, in addition to an annual administrative fee of $500 or the amount necessary to cover Caltrans' actual cost." In this vein the group occupied 66 Berry Street, a house owned by Caltrans. The occupation brought attention to SB-120 and to the proposed Giant's baseball stadium next to that property. Though the squatters claimed that the house should be rented out, Caltrans argued that the land was excess property and was therefore exempt from the law, though Caltrans stated that it would sell the building to the city for market value. The Board of Supervisors, as well as Homes Not Jails activists, supported this plan, but Jordan refused to purchase the building.

Making the private public? Antagonistic politics and squatting in San Francisco

These anarchist understandings of squatting suggest that it is an inherently radical act; it confronts the sanctity of private property and, through direct action, houses homeless residents. In addition, squatting frees people from the tyranny of rent, allowing them to spend their time working on political activism and the creation of a do-it-yourself culture. If squatting were a radical act, it would have been treated as such by mayor Jordan, a politician who was chiefly concerned with maintaining order, and was a strong friend to land developers and housing associations, but that didn't happen. Jordan did go after activists with Homes Not Jails, and many of their actions resulted in large numbers of arrests and public haranguing by the mayor, but many other actions were ignored. What helps us unravel the differential treatment by the mayor towards Homes Not Jails' actions?

First, Jordan's driving concern was the creation and maintenance of public order, clearing the streets of the homeless for the sake of business and changing the city's reputation as a magnet city for the homeless, as argued in the last chapter. For this reason, I contend that the covert squatting actions of Homes Not Jails did not bother Jordan nearly as much did the public feedings of Food Not Bomb, since covert squatting is an inherently private matter, and was framed as a civil—not criminal—problem.

The private nature of squatting played, to some degree, into the hands of the mayor. Since Jordan sought to remove the homeless from public view, without using social services or government aid, Homes Not Jails can be seen as inadvertently supporting Jordan's plan. The group removed up to 500 homeless people a night from the parks and streets by placing them within private, albeit illegal squats.[8] This explains why the only times that Jordan or the police spoke out against the group, or mass arrested members of the group, were during public actions, or while the group was in the process of trying to gain legal title to a building—such as what happened to squatters who occupied federal or Caltrans property. These public actions received quick reactions from the administration and an uncompromising stance from the mayor. One example, discussed earlier, was the mayor's reluctance to accept the federal government's offer to purchase a building from them for well below market price. This property was in the heart of Jordan's China Basin redevelopment plan, and for this and other reasons, Jordan was hostile to the idea of having a dedicated homeless shelter in that section of town. The question of gentrifying the China Basin district had not been that important in the public media, and the action by Homes Not Jails forced that issue back into the media debate. These public actions questioned the mayor's ability to maintain public order and ensure the protection of private property.

The public squats and public feedings both politicized the private, and broke down the division between private and public. Covert squatting did not do this, but instead reinforced the public/private divide, removing the homeless from the public eye and making them no longer a public concern. Public actions, on the other hand, politicized housing, and radically questioned the mayor's stance against city-funded affordable housing programs.

Covert squatting nonetheless served an important function, as it allowed the group to house as many people as possible. As mentioned earlier, the group opened up hundreds of covert squats and housed well over a thousand people over a six-year period. These are significant numbers, regardless of whether or not they drew the ire of Frank Jordan's administration. In fact, Homes Not Jails can be viewed as a substantial success. One difficulty inherent in anarchist social justice direct action—from Food Not Bombs and Homes Not Jails to anarchist Free Schools—is the tension between conflicting with the powers to be and the push to provide needed social services, since oftentimes these objectives are mutually exclusive. Food Not Bombs, for instance, constantly had to make decisions regarding which is more important—the arrests, confronting Jordan publicly, and gaining media attention to homeless issues, or feeding as many hungry people as possible. This tension between providing what homeless people urgently need was often contrasted with the groups' ability to disrupt the powers that be. For Homes Not Jails, this tension was made even more difficult by the fact that adverse possession laws force the squatting to open, which, as Roy notes, makes adverse possession much less likely to occur. Thus Homes Not Jails had to decide whether providing short-term housing for the homeless was more important than attempting to gain property through openly occupying a location. This all being said, the reaction of Jordan to Homes Not Jails also highlights the fact that covert squatting is not nearly as large a threat to the established order as one might think.

The second key reason for the deferential treatment towards Homes Not Jails is that Homes Not Jails might have been providing benefits (all be it marginal) for housing values in San Francisco. According to property law scholars Eduardo Moisés Peñalver and Sonia K. Katyal in *Property outlaws: how squatters, pirates, and protests improve the law of ownership*, the authors contend, counter-intuitively, that property outlaws are essential to solidifying and strengthening property law. They state:

> Not all disobedience, even the acquisitive variety, need contribute to a sense of widespread disorder that would undermine broader crime-control efforts. An act of illegal appropriation may actually contribute to visible order ... A great deal of urban squatting in the United States in the 1970s and 1980s was highly organized and likewise may have worked to displace the preexisting disorder generated by extensive urban abandonment. Urban squatters were fixing broken windows, not breaking them. (Peñalver and Katyal, 2010: 133)

In the author's analysis of urban squatting in the United States and elsewhere, squatters do not shatter the image of social and public order, but often promote it. Thus "urban squatters were fixing broken windows, not breaking them" by literally taking abandoned houses and replacing broken windows, painting, and cleaning up the yard. For these reasons, the authors believe that squatters strengthen, not weaken, public order, private property rights, and housing values.

This analysis is also noted by Hans Prujt who states; "under a market-oriented urban regime, improvements made by citizens to run down neighborhoods (for example by fixing up abandoned buildings and chasing drug dealers from the streets, or by creating a community garden in an empty lot) can attract property developers" (Pruijt, 2003: 148). This is why one of the New York squatters he quoted quipped "squatters are the real storm troopers of gentrification" (Pruijt, 2003: 148). Thus by taking abandoned and unused homes and buildings and occupying them, squatters can breathe life into a neighborhood, decreasing the visible signs of disorder, and actually improve housing values.

In this regard the sweat equity of Homes Not Jails, which is supposed to help homeless people gain access to a building via adverse possession, also makes them easily exploitable. Cities can, as Roy pointed out, create an exploitable relationship between private property owners and squatters. In this relationship, the squatters can put a large amount of labor and resources into an abandoned house, drastically improving the building's value and be evicted before they gain rights under the law. Thus landlords can exploit the labor of the homeless, get tax write-offs for the building, and sell the building for a profit.

Overall, then, the apparent reasons that Frank Jordan did not harass Homes Not Jails to the same degree that he did Food Not Bombs was that covert squatting, an inherently private enterprise, helps remove the most visible homeless from the streets, thus accomplishing Jordan's greatest desire. He sought to hide the homeless from the public—creating a city that was a safe space for middle-class residents, corporations, businesses, and tourists. Homes Not Jails actually helped Jordan's agenda by fixing the broken windows that frustrated the Jordan Administration.

At the same time, the public takeovers highlighted the group's confrontational and antagonistic relationship with the city by applying pressure to address housing issues. In addition, around Thanksgiving and Christmas each year, the group could refocus issues of housing and the creative actions of the homeless community. Through public takeovers they, put pressure on Caltrans and the city to follow state and federal law, which mandated that unused government buildings be used to house the homeless. A tension existed between social service and confrontational dimensions of the group. Within this tension the group moved to put more energy and effort into providing housing, rather than public protest and outrage.

Conclusion

The lesson we can learn from the dedication, hard work, and militant energy of Homes Not Jails is that political activism and ethical action makes for complicated decisions. The primary lesson we can learn from mayor Jordan's differential treatment of covert and public squatting actions is that in the neoliberal city, the management and control of public space is of the utmost importance. The public actions of Homes Not Jails, similar to the public actions of Food Not Bombs, resulted in a draconian reaction from the city. Since Jordan was so concerned with the optics of order and security, anything that shattered that image resulted in such a response. His lack of aggressive reaction to the more covert squats adds additional evidence and support for this claim. When Homes Not Jails housed the homeless, the mayor seemed much less concerned that their illegal action would undermine his administration. This is because his primary concern was not the concept of liberal property relations, but instead the defining of public space in such a way as to facilitate gentrification.

This is not to discount the hard work and important function that Homes Not Jails' covert actions had on the lived experiences of the houseless and poor in San Francisco. When we think of anarchist politics, we tend to focus on the public resistance and antagonistic politics that occur between radical activists and the police. This is not just a result of the fetishization of conflict and violence, even though conflict and struggle is often a core component of political change. But people are not pawns in the game of revolution. This tension within anarchist politics between antagonism and mutual aid is brought to the fore with both Food Not Bombs and, as this chapter clearly shows, Homes Not Jails. When it comes to Homes Not Jails their covert actions, which did not receive the aggressive response from the city, housed up to 500 people on a given night. This has to be seen as a huge success, and though it did not bring about the end of capitalism, neither did the more antagonistic actions. Instead of viewing antagonism as the goal, it is important to understand both sides as essential components of the anarchist push for radical urban change. As Bakunin famously said: "The destructive urge is also a creative urge." The flip side might also be said: "the creation of alternative institutions is also a destructive urge."

Notes

1   Geographies of survival are places formed by the dispossessed and marginalized to engage in acts, often illegally, that are needed for their survival. In this study, Food Not Bombs is forming a space, the public feedings, in which a needed act (eating) is done. Likewise, squatting is an act of survival in which a homeless person illegally takes over a house in order to get access to shelter.
2   Of all the major cities in the United States, New York City is the most squatter-friendly environment, since the city has absurdly high rental costs and a large number of vacant housing units. However, the city tried to change this during the 1980s and 1990s, intentionally destroying large numbers of their vacant housing stock in what many feel was an attempt to decrease their vacancy rate and raise the rental price of units.
3   The German autonomous squatters are responsible for developing the black bloc tactic which has become central to anarchist mass protest actions.
4   The autonomous Marxist movement in Europe shares many similarities to the anarchist movement today. Though many autonomists from the 1980s did not refer to themselves as anarchists but as "autonomous Marxists," since the 1990s autonomists have come closer to self-identifying as anarchists. That being said, Antonio Negri, a well-known autonomist Marxist theorist has always refused to call himself an anarchist. In Empire, Michael Hardt and Antonio Negri openly state their hostility to anarchism, which they associate with naivety and sporadic acts of violence, even though Negri promotes a stateless form of communism that is anti-authority and anti-hierarchy, and is organized around direct democracy.
5   There is an intense irony in the city spending $100,000 in an attempt to convict four activists for occupying a house, when that money could have been spent housing a very large number of homeless residents.
6   Food Not Bombs did have support, at times, on the Board of Supervisors, most notably with Angela Alioto, but they never worked with Board members in drafting legislation, and were never invited to speak at Board meetings. Homes Not Jails both helped to draft legislation and was allowed space to talk. Part of this is the result of the involvement of Ted Gullickson, from the San Francisco Tenant Union's. Gullickson was a well-known figure in the

housing rights movement and was well connected with the more liberal
elements of San Francisco politics.

7   The other major federal land occupation by the group was in 1996 and 1997
    when the group occupied the Presidio military base. The base was being
    closed and the city planned to tear down the 900 houses on the base to
    develop them into up-scale housing. The group protested against this plan,
    arguing that the 900 houses should be used as affordable low-income housing.
    The public occupations by the group, and Religious Witness, were successful,
    as the housing units were turned into low-income housing.

8   While the 500 persons a night for Homes Not Jails might seem relatively
    small in comparison to the 10,000 or so homeless people in the city, the
    number is quite impressive and relatively large considering the barely 5,000
    beds available through government funded shelters. Overall, at most, Homes
    Not Jails housed about 10% of the remaining homeless in the city.

7

Towards an anarchist "right to the city"

I participated in my first major protest in 2001, shortly after the United States military started the invasion of Afghanistan. In the days before the invasion started, activist groups all over the city of Des Moines were meeting, coordinating, and planning. Groups organized their own actions, but collectively we were going to take the streets of downtown Des Moines. We planned to show the power of the people and voice our massive opposition to the death machine being put in motion by George W. Bush, Cheney, and their cronies. I cannot remember how many people showed up, but to me it seemed like thousands. It was clear to me that a revolution was at hand, and that we were going to stop this damn war! I was caught up in the excitement of the moment and thought we could conquer the world. Instead of thousands, it was probably only a few hundred; instead of stopping the war, the anti-war movement fizzled out and the occupation continues to this day.

At that first protest (and nearly every protest I have ever attended since) we all shouted, with passion and rage:

Whose streets? OUR STREETS!!!
Whose streets? OUR STREETS?

Considering that the few hundred of us holding signs and papier-mâché puppets were facing down both a well-armed police force and a handful of right-wing counter protests, "we knew we were making impossible demands." We had the streets for the moment, but the second our permit was up or the police decided enough was enough, we would lose control of those streets. The dream would be kept alive though: an urban space in which the people controlled the streets, the housing, and economy. We demanded not because it might be given to us, but because to merely demand is to exercise power.

At this moment, with the rise of right-wing populism and neo-fascist organizing, the flawed election of Donald Trump, the near-complete corporate takeover of the Democratic Party, and the militarization of the police, winning might seem impossible. But, as I hope the rest of this book has shown, where there is oppression there is also resistance. And where there is resistance there is reason for change. Such resistance was in short supply during the Obama administration. The issue is not that there was no oppression, or that urban life was idyllic during Obama's administration but there is a massive difference between Obama's neoliberal politics and the far right authoritarianism of the Trump administration. One of the effects of neoliberalism is that it blurs the distinction between oppressors and oppressed by disconnecting individuals from one another, creating policy in a historical vacuum, and monetizing all aspects of life. Recently we also saw a melding of neoliberalism with identity politics and even intersectionality, as Hillary Clinton's campaign often used the language of both to court the left to her side. The net impact of, hopefully late, state neoliberalism is that the causes of oppression became so decentralized and so hidden that it was increasingly hard to organize effectively against it. We saw the intentional muddying of the understood dichotomy of enemy/friend relations. Neoliberals learned what activists have known for a long time: it is hard to fight against a decentralized enemy.

With Trump in the White House, things are looking much different. The lines are being clearly drawn, both by activists and the Trump administration. For example, his racial attacks on immigrants have led to revivals of the sanctuary movement, and his plans to register Muslims have led to more alliances between Jewish and Muslim groups than we have seen in many years. The left has something that it has not had since G. W. Bush—an enemy—and with an identifiable enemy, the left has the passion, direction, and potential unity needed to effect radical change. Will it happen? Who knows, but right now the dream I had as a nineteen-year-old in the streets for the first time is coming back to me; thousands of Americans are now experiencing the spirit of revolt for the very first time. It is time for us to occupy everything—streets, schools, government buildings, parks, pipelines—and to learn to make demands again:

To demand not just higher wages, but the end of capitalism;
To demand not just debt-free college, but the elimination of all debt;
To demand not just the continuation of DACA (Deferred Action of Childhood Arrivals), but the elimination of borders;
To demand not just the streets, but the entire city!

I want to focus on the demand for a right to the city in this chapter. My goal is to put the experience and ideas that we have explored through the rest of the book into dialogue with the academic work and activist demands

currently made around the right to the city. My assertion is that by centralizing the experiences of urban anarchism and homeless resistance, we can
begin a more nuanced and complicated discussion around autonomy, public/
private spaces, and urban anti-capitalism.

Whose streets? The theoretical and historical dimensions of the right to the city

> The actual existing Right to the City, as it is now constituted, is far too
> narrowly confined, in most cases in the hands of a small political and
> economic elite who are in position to shape the city more and more after
> their own particular needs and hearts' desire. (Harvey, 2013: 24)

San Francisco, like most major urban spaces in the world, has increasingly
become a plaything for the rich: within this context, concepts like quality
of life gain their class-war dimension. When a city politician calls to protect
or expand quality of life, they are primarily concerned with the lives of the
elite and do not care about access to housing, or health care, or food, unless
the lack of these resources impacts the quality of life of the tourist and
urban upper-crusters. This is why there is a need to theorize a grassroots,
anti-capitalist right to the city.

The slogan "a right to the city" was coined by the radical urban geog-
rapher Henri Lefebvre and has since grown into a battle cry for urban
movements around the globe. In making this call Lefebvre wrote that:

> These rights, which are not well recognized, progressively become cus-
> tomary before being inscribed into formalized codes. They would change
> reality if they entered into social practice: right to work, to training and
> education, to health, housing, leisure, to life. Among these rights in the
> making feature the right to the city, not to the ancient city, but to urban
> life, to renew centrality, to places of encounter and exchange, to life
> rhythms and time uses, enabling the full and complete usage of these
> moments and places, etc. (Lefebvre, 1996: 178).

In effect, Lefebvre was demanding the rethinking of urban space and the
creation of it through a new collective social order. The social nature of this
right is, as David Harvey notes, important to highlight, as it is an example
of radicalizing the language of rights, and turning them from being individual in nature to being the enabling conditions for collective life and
political contestation.

Of course demanding a right to the city is not a new concept or desire.
One of the most important anarchist moments—the Paris Commune of

7.1 Food Not Bombs Don't Cop Out flier, 1989

1871—should be seen as an urban revolt against the elite: radical re-envisioning of urban life from below. The political and economic order of urban spaces has obviously changed since then and, as such, a new version of their demands needs to be developed. This new version of the right to the city has to reflect an understanding of the globalized economic context of modern capitalism; it has to engage the class and racial dynamics that exist within urban and rural and suburban spaces; and it needs to contextualize itself within an ever changing global climate and environment.

What are the politics that emerge from the contemporary right to the city? According to David Harvey, one of the most influential theorists connected to the concept, it is first essential to understand the role that urban space plays in the construction of the modern capitalist economy. To Harvey, the processes of mass urbanization is directly connected to the cycles of contemporary capitalism and has become one of the primary locations used by contemporary capitalism to re-accumulate capital and wealth. It is for this reason that, to Harvey, the urban needs to be seen as a central node of contemporary anti-capitalist politics and also why urban revolts and uprisings tend to interweave urban concerns with broader class ones. In seeing the urban as playing such a central role, Harvey sees the construction of a socialist alternative, both locally and more broadly, as having to engage with the urban question.

At the local level Harvey calls for: 1) the protection and expansion of urban commons; 2) the strengthening of local labor networks; and 3) the creation of local and direct involvement of people in the management of the city. All three of these broad politics are rooted in providing working people with the ability to manipulate and alter the development of the urban space (Harvey, 2013). This is essential because the structure of urban life not only produces the city, but also produces the qualities of the residents that live there. What does this mean? It means—following Marx's claim (Tucker, 1978: 4) that "It is not the consciousness of men that determines their being, but, on the contrary, their social being that determines their consciousness"—that the neoliberal city not only constructs space in a certain way, but also shapes and alters the relationships between people, alters the economic base of a city, and alters the social and psychological ways in which we engage with the world around us. By expanding labor networks, protecting the commons, and creating outlets for participatory planning and managing the common people, not just the rich, the people will gain the ability to shape the city towards their own ends. As the socialist city develops, and engages with the global economic world, it can, hopefully, spark a series of revolts and similar projects. Harvey writes that "the Right to the City has to be construed not as a right to that which already exists, but as a right to rebuild and re-create the city as a socialist body politic in a completely different image" (Harvey, 2013: 138). This tension between the present and the future city provides the space for urban insurrection and radical social movements.

During the 2004 and 2005 World Social Forum, a network of urban groups throughout the world came together and drafted the "World Charter for the Right to the City" (hereafter WCRC). This document asserts that: "The Right to the City broadens the traditional focus on improvement of peoples' quality of life based on housing and the neighborhood" and defines the right to the city as "the equitable usufruct of cities within the principles of sustainability, democracy, equity and social justice" (World Social Forum, 2005). By looking to develop a broader understanding of rights and protections for urban residents, the document's goal is to construct a world in which "all people may live with dignity in our cities" (World Social Forum, 2005).

The document calls for a radical reimagining of the urban landscape and enshrines both collective and individual rights that go beyond the basic liberal protections that are often at the core of contemporary politics. In the WCRC, we can see the authors developing an urban politics that centers rights around: economic justice, democratic participation, and the guarantee of basic needs. The development of rights in these aspects of social life are essential for moving the city to where "the public and private spaces and goods of the city and its citizens should be used prioritizing social, cultural, and environmental interests" (World Social Forum, 2005).

In addition to the development of basic economic, cultural, and human rights, the document also centralized the most vulnerable in society. The authors argue that city resources should be used to provide services, first and foremost, to those experiencing extreme poverty, violence, medical needs, or natural disasters, and to refugees and migrants. Implicit in this list would be homeless residents. Beyond this call for supporting the vulnerable first, the only right expressly guaranteed to the homeless in the WCRC is:

> All homeless citizens, individually, as couples, or as family groups, have the right to demand of the authorities effective implementation of their right to adequate housing in a progressive manner and through application of all available resources. Shelter and bed-and-breakfast facilities may be adopted as provisional emergency measures, without obviating the obligation to provide definitive housing solutions. (World Social Forum, 2005).

This is an essential and important right for the homeless and, when combined with the guarantee to all residents of basic human needs—food, clothing, shelter, and medical care—forms a powerful call for justice.

In order to promote and develop the right to the city, the WCRC calls for a concerted effort made up of social movements, government agencies, and international organizations. In practice, it is social movements, a politics of disruption, and the actions of urban groups that have been the backbone of the agitation for the right to the city. This is the case with the Right to the City Alliance, the largest right to the city coalition in the United States, which is a:

> unified response to gentrification and a call to halt the displacement of low-income people, people of color, marginalized LGBTQ communities,

and youths of color from their historic urban neighborhoods. We are a national alliance of racial, economic and environmental justice organizations. (Right to the City Alliance, n.d.)

This alliance, which has been in place since 2007, coordinates a range of groups and social movements around the concept of a right to the city. The groups in the coalition use a range of tactics—from electoral politics, to educational efforts, to non-violent protests, and to direct action. This diversity of groups and tactics is essential for highlighting that a broad range of groups exist within this wider movement for a right to the city; with diversity of tactics also comes ideological diversity.

What we see with the intellectual work of David Harvey, on the one hand, and the political work of the WCRC, and the right to the city Alliance, on the other, is a complex urban politics. It is an urban politics that looks to reimagine the city, moving it away from the neoliberal logic that currently governs cities, to a socialist politics. This socialist politics centers on the economic, cultural, and political needs of the economically vulnerable and seeks to expand democratic spaces for participation. In guaranteeing the right to basic needs, democratic participation, and access to city resources, the Right to City movement confronts the primary structural barriers to urban justice and also provides empowering outlets for individuals and groups to be political, empowered, and engaged.

Are there tent-cities in our utopian future? Centralizing the homeless in the right to the city

As the above discussion hopefully shows, I am a believer and defender of the idea of a right to the city. As a concept, and as a political movement, it provides space and opportunity for a radical, and potentially revolutionary, urban politics. It also claims to centralize the needs of the most vulnerable, which, in following the first chapter, is a core value within what I call an anarchist homelessness politics. That being said, there is still space for friendly criticism and critical engagement. In this section I want to refocus the conversation around what lessons the right to the city might teach, focusing on anarchist homeless movements. In going back to the first chapter, by taking the anarchist homeless perspective—which both understands the homeless as victims of global capitalist systems of oppression and also as politically powerful actors who make legitimate personal and collective decisions—an alternative right to the city is constructed that focuses on complicating the right to the city's productionist core, and queering their conceptions of public space.

Against productionism: work refusal, the abolition of work, and the right to work

Recently I saw a meme on Facebook that stated: "you do not hate Mondays, you hate capitalism." The sardonic comment, like all good humor, has more than a kernel of truth in it. Increasingly, polling data has been coming out showing that the majority of American's dislike their job. A 2013 National Gallop poll found that only 30% of Americans enjoy going to work; over 50% do not enjoy their jobs; and nearly 20% completely hate going to work (Grant, 2013). This dislike of work conflicts with the concept of the Protestant work ethic and the overall American myth of bootstrapping which is commonly associated with hard work. According to the theoretical and historical work developed by scholars associated with the autonomous Marxist school of thought, we go to work because social, economic, and political forces are constantly pressuring us to accept both the ideological logic of work, while coercive forces punish us if we do not.

Expanding on the work of E. P. Thompson (1966), autonomist Marxists remind us that the worker is not a natural concept, but those in power are constantly producing us into workers through policy and ideological domination. Providing additional historical analysis of this process, Peter Linebaugh and Marcus Rediker (2013), in *The many-headed hydra*, provides a powerful and provocative history of early American colonists and their relationships with labor and work. In this book the authors provide a comprehensive overview of the many ways in which the refusal of work—by either work stoppages or by fleeing the colonies for maroon communities— as well as a culture of sloth and laziness, was repressed and defeated by those in power. Expanding on the basic critique of work, Selma James (2012), Silvia Federici (2012), and others within the wages for housework movement, show that what we consider work in the modern economy is narrowly defined in such a way as to remove most of the exploited labor that occurs. The labor of (mostly) women at home, and other required acts of social reproduction, are excluded from the category, and therefore are completely uncompensated. It was in his engagement with the work of these great feminist scholars and activists that George Caffentzis had his idea of work and labor shaken: "I have seen the world of objects as products of an intertwined struggle between work and its refusal and every person's actions as being either work for capital (or preparation for it) or its refusal" (Caffentzis, 2013: 8).

What we can see from the discussion above is an analysis of work that understands the process as a dialectic between work and refusal. Every day I go to work and the forces and tensions that promote work push against me, as do the desires and wants within me to refuse to work—to stay home, do the labor that makes me happy, and enjoy my life. By understanding this

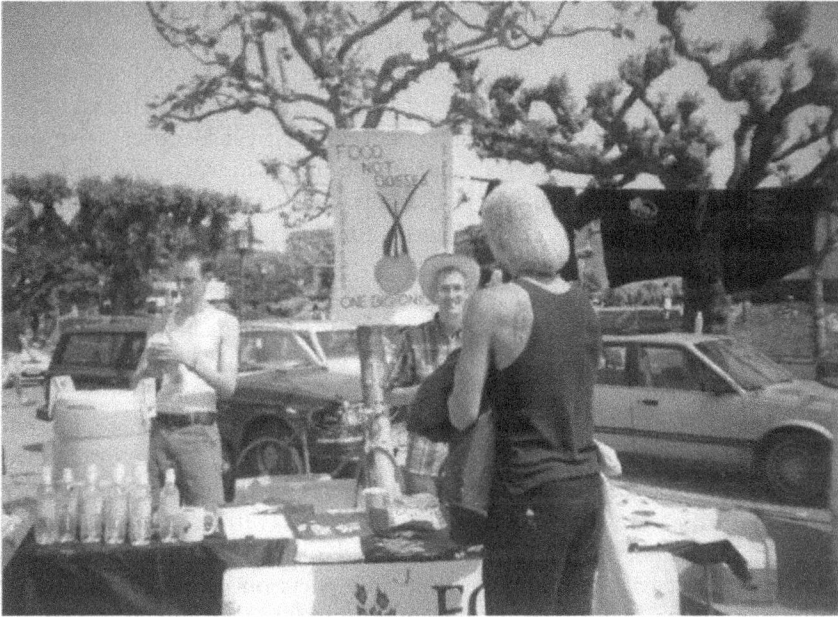

7.2 Food Not Boss, IWWW and Food Not Bombs Collaboration 1995

process we can remove the idea that working is a natural thing for people to do, and instead see work as a political topic.

Theoretically, when discussing the right to the city, Harvey focuses on the producers within the city—broadly defined. In explaining this he writes:

> It [the right to the city] is inclusive not only of construction workers but also all of those who facilitate the reproduction of daily life: the care-givers and teachers, the sewer and subway repairmen, the plumbers and electricians, the scaffold erectors and crane operators, the hospital workers and the truck, bus, and taxi drivers, the restaurant workers and the entertainers, the bank clerks and the city administrators. (Harvey, 2013: 137)

This list, while extensive, focuses only on a certain form of city resident—the producer; what is not mentioned (in this list or the entire book) are the homeless. By refocusing the right to the city towards the homeless, the productionist aspects of most socialist politics becomes clear. This is not to say that the homeless do not labor and work, because they clearly do. Anyone who has struggled to survive extreme poverty knows how much work and energy goes into it. But the homeless are often defined by their lack of economic productivity. People do not see the hunting and gathering, the time spent negotiating the service institutions, and other acts of survival, as economically productive. It is through denying the work of the homeless, that the idea that work will set them free is able to emerge. This is, as the first chapter discussed, the argument developed by neoconservative and neoliberal thinkers. They believe that freedom and independence is found through work. Socialists should not, in any way, parrot the logic here. Yet one of the major sections in the Charter for the right to the city is on the right to work.

In this section, in which the authors are attempting to reclaim the phrase from the right, they develop a policy of full employment. In their proposal, all should be able to work, and barriers to work should be addressed. For example, childcare should be provided so parents can work, and facilities should be developed to allow the disabled to work. The logic here, following a Marxist reading of objectification—the idea that who we are is defined by what we produce—centralizes work as being of the utmost importance for social and individual good. This is not to say that expanding labor protections, democratizing workplaces, and other radical socialist labor projects do not have profoundly positive impacts on people's lives, but to only focus on the right to work does not go nearly far enough.

This idea of a leftist conception of a right to work needs to be drastically expanded to include labor that is not currently included as productive. In addition, there needs to be a secondary right: "a right to leisure." The vision for this right can even be found within the work of Marx himself, who wrote:

> For as soon as the distribution of labour comes into being, each man has a particular exclusive sphere of activity, which is forced upon him and from which he cannot escape. He is a hunter, a fisherman, a shepherd, or a critical critic and must remain so if he does not wish to lose his means of livelihood; while in communist society, where nobody has one exclusive sphere of activity but each can become accomplished in any branch he wishes, society regulates the general production and thus makes it possible for me to do one thing today and another tomorrow, to hunt in the morning, to fish in the afternoon, rear cattle in the evening, criticize after dinner, just as I have in mind, without ever becoming hunter, fisherman, shepherd or critic. (Tucker, 1978: 160)

The primary lesson from the argument above is that when we centralize our concerns around economic production, many forms of labor are excluded from the social calculation. Women's domestic labor is excluded, the immaterial labor of all of us who produce culture are excluded, and the underground economies and acts of survival of the homeless are as well. This exclusion can be seen within the Charter above when it comes to child

raising. The charter calls for the production of childcare centers and providing parents access to that service, but does not call for wages for housework
or to pay parents for raising children. Instead, only the formal economic
labor of a childcare worker is considered productive economic work. By
focusing on a critique of what we consider work and economic production,
we open space to think differently and focus on forms of labor that we
otherwise ignore. By supporting these forms of labor, and viewing them as
valuable, we also provide more space for people to spend their time and
energy working on the projects and topics that give them the most meaning.

By refocusing away from work to leisure, the right to the city can expand
on and centralize happiness and individual autonomy. This focus on enjoy-
ment is also essential in a world on the brink of ecological catastrophe. At
the current moment, what is needed is not a growth economy, or an expansion of industrial production, but a degrowth economy. As long as the focus
is on work and production, there is no real space to contract the economy
in the way that is needed. Focusing on leisure and free time allows this. A
socialism that does not focus on leisure is not really fighting for the wants
of the working class and is not addressing the scope of the ecological crises
we are facing. Workers, and non-workers, of the world . . . take the day off!

Public space as commons: rethinking public space and the right to the city

The majority of this book has been about the importance of theorizing and
understanding public space and the role that space plays in resisting gentrification and state power. By focusing on the homeless, questions of public
space are more complicated than if we had focused on other social issues.
Since the homeless spend the majority of their time living in public space—
making the public space also their private space—it is not a location that
they use only to make political demands but, as their homes, also a location
that they must defend against state encroachment. The work within the
right to the city understands rather well the first point—that public space
is a central location for political engagement—but are much less clear about
the second point.

According to the Charter, "All persons have the right to associate, meet,
and manifest themselves. Cities should provide and guarantee public spaces
for this effect" (World Social Forum, 2005). This protection, which is essential for politics to emerge and develop within a city, is a huge step towards
reimaging public space as the political agora it used to be. This understanding of public space as an essential location for social movement and political
organizing is seen within the work of many scholars of public space. For
instance, Don Mitchell writes that "Representation, whether of oneself or

7.3 Public meal at Soupstock, 2000

of a group, demands space" (Mitchell, 2003: 33). If our ability to represent ourselves requires access to public space, then defense of space is essential for the creation of a vibrant and cohesive urban life.

This understanding of democratic public space works relatively well when you are talking about groups and individuals temporarily using public space for personal projects or for occupation for political reasons. But when you bring in the homeless question, this dynamic becomes more complicated and the politics more conflictual. The majority of work on the right to the city avoids engaging in the complex politics of homelessness and only pays quick lip service. Likewise, nearly all value the protection of making public space a commons. In this section I want to put the two together and think about public space as a commons, and what that means for homeless residents of a city.

Since the Zapatista uprising in 1994 there has been a resurgence in left thinking around the concept of the commons, especially among those connected to Autonomous Marxism. For instance, Peter Linebaugh (2009) in *The Magna Carta Manifesto*, calls on the left to go back to an embrace of the charter of forests, found in the Magna Carta, which provided the peasants of Europe legal right to common forest and grazing lands. The commons served as an important space within feudal society. They served as an economic buffer, allowing peasants additional ways to gain access to food and other resources, and also served as a location to organize and resist the feudal powers. For instance, the mythic figure, Robin Hood, who was a thorn in the side of the British nobility, organized, and fought, out of the common forestland, and used that as a base of operation. His resistance was also tied to fighting against the English attempts to enclose the commons. If we expand the concept of the commons to any collectively shared resource that we all have access to, we can imagine not just forestland, but physical, virtual, and economic spaces that exist all around us—from public space, to cultural commons, to shared economic resources. In all cases, Linebaugh warns against the attempt to enclosure and privatize these commons, which can be done via the privatization of public space, the zoning of it for specific consumer activities, and the exclusion of people.

The theoretical defense of enclosure is most accurately described in the seminal article "The Tragedy of the Commons." In this piece, Garrett Hardin argues that commons are inherently unstable spaces and that the forces of human nature and capitalism are guaranteed to destroy them. In making this argument, he asks us to imagine a common field, in which everyone can bring their sheep to graze. If there is no barrier to entrance, no fee, and no regulation, each person will have the incentive to maximize the amount of land and sheep that they can bring to the commons. Doing so allows them to maximize their money. If everyone did this, the field would be severely over grazed, and within a short period of time would no longer ecologically function. The solution, in Hardin's estimation, is to privatize the land and sell the commons to each rancher. The logic being that each rancher, now that they have ownership of the piece of land, will, due to self-interest, be better stewards of the land. In effect, he is arguing that within a commons there is an incentive for every person to take and use the resource more and not give back, or take care of it (Hardin, 1968).

While there have been many arguments against "The Tragedy of the Commons," most notably by Nobel prize winner Eleanor Ostrom (1990), in the modern era of neoliberalism, the dominant logic of the government has been to sell or gift public commons to private owners and corporations. Constructing and developing a socialistic understanding, the city will work to stop this enclosure and open that space up for public use again. Access to the commons, then, need to be thought of as a right for all to use, and it is a right that is directly tied to need. So, for instance, this means the right of the homeless to turn public space into tent-cities. This view goes against the conservative idea of quality of life, which views tent-cities and homeless encampments as limiting the access of other residents to use parks and public space. In making that argument, the conservatives do not take into account aspects of power and questions of need. When we think of a commons, we need to understand that certain people and groups have greater needs to access resources from the commons. The homeless, for instance, need access to basic housing and spaces to live their lives. Since much of the world has been privatized, and they are excluded, this leaves only the commons of public space. By centralizing need and vulnerability we can prioritize public space for use by those with the most need.

In addition, by focusing on the needs of the homeless, we need to think about public space differently—mostly in collapsing the border between private and public. The general idea of the commons, at its core, does not adhere to a public/private dichotomy, as the commons were both public spaces and also spaces for the maintenance of basic human needs. If anything, the liberal conception of the public/private is rooted, at least in some part, in the enclosure of the commons and the state regulation and management of public space that developed in the last few hundred centuries. The homeless, due to their lack of a private realm of life, need to live their life in public. This is often disallowed as it is seen as a corruption of the public realm. We see this in Hannah Arendt's (1998) *On the human condition*, where she warns about bringing in the values of the *homo economicus* into the public realm and, more clearly, by city laws banning sleeping, urinating, defecating, and other basic human needs in public space. Centralizing the needs of the homeless within public space means a rethinking of this dualism and an open embrace of the satisfaction of all basic human needs in public. This is already the case for most middle- and upper-class park users, who can have a nice picnic lunch or a nap in the sun without a citation for illegal camping and eating.

In viewing public space as a commons and understanding that a commons does not adhere to the public/private divide, parks and other spaces become complicated and unique spaces in which leisure, survival, and politics meld together. The interaction between these different parts of life blurs boundaries in ways that undermine the liberal concern with separate spheres of life. Under capitalism, we work at our work place, we relax at our homes, and we engage in politics in public (or the voting booth). Of course, even in practice this is not the case. In recent decades, the realm of work has started to colonize the other as most of us think about, or engage at work in home, and, with the corporatization of politics, our political choices are increasingly linked with either work or consumption. By believing that these aspects of our lives are different, we attempt to quarantine them from each other, and in doing so obfuscate the links that exist between them all. Focusing on homeless residents, and reimagining public space as a commons, allows us to break down these walls and realize that our leisure, work, surivival, and politics are all one and the same.

Urban revolts in the era of Trump

I am writing this in the early period of the Trump administration: already we have seen a huge overreach by the Trump administration, with executive orders banning immigrants from many Muslim nations, an assault on immigrants and sanctuary cities, and a massive shake up of government. In addition to these attacks on poor people, immigrants, and other groups, we have seen a huge push back. The resistance began on day one as protestors disrupted aspects of the inauguration and black bloc protestors took to the streets of DC. The day after the election, over 3 million people throughout the nation protested against the Trump administration during the Women's March. The ban of Muslim immigrants and refugees led to massive protests at airports throughout the nation. In Flagstaff, a city far from a major airport hub, over 500 people showed up to protest against the ban. In a similar fashion, the executive order against sanctuary cities has resulted in massive opposition from urban centers—as places like San Francisco, LA, Seattle, and Boston—have declared their intentions to remain sanctuaries, and the Governor of California, Jerry Brown, has promised that California will lead the state opposition to the Trump administration.

It is not surprising that cities have become one of the main sites of resistance to the current administration. With the exception of Phoenix, every major urban center voted strongly against Donald Trump, and it is clear that one of the main dividing lines that Trump used to take power was the urban–suburban/rural divide. This has been a long-time conservative approach to populism, though, as republicans like Ted Cruz have spoken out against "New York values" and how "San Franciscan" has become a slur on conservative talk radio. Increasingly, though, the United States, like the rest of the world, is urbanizing. In the United States, this growth is mostly in the middle-sized cities. From 2000–2010 cities between 500,000 and a million people grew at 24.8%, while the nation, on average, only grew at 9.7%. As people increasingly move towards cities, and rural and suburban populations lag behind them, the divide between the two will continue to grow.

In the Trump era, we can imagine cities continuing to grow as spaces of resistance, and the struggle between the federal government, conservative state legislatures, and cities to intensify. That said, urban spaces have become central to the political economy of the country, as well as the world, and are also locations in which massive unrest and disruption has the power to undermine regional, state, and even international economies. The more that cities become the location of rebellion, the more the idea of a right to the city is needed as a means to radicalize urban politics, and in effect, the national base for the political resistance. In this battle for the soul and material base of cities, the homeless have an important role to play. They are not the only revolutionary class within current urban life, but they are definitely one of them.

Coda: theses on homelessness, public space, and urban resistance

Have you ever seen a 6-foot tall person in an owl costume lock themselves to the doors of a bank? I know I have, and it is a beautiful and majestic sight. In the mid-2000s, while protesting against old growth logging in Oregon, hundreds of environmental activists took to the streets and blockaded a public entrance to the "stumpqua" bank's downtown office. The protestors were putting pressure on the bank to divest, as the bank was, and still is, connected to some of the largest logging corporations in the northwest, corporations that were being gifted heavily subsidized public old growth lands to log. Not surprisingly, shortly after shutting down the bank—making it impossible to get in or out—the police showed up to arrest the owl locking down. It was here that the magic happened. The protestors must have studied under David Copperfield because after having the lockdown devices broken the protestors surrounded the owl and . . . poof! He disappeared.

Hegel famously wrote, "The owl of Minerva spreads its wings only with the falling of the dusk." The owl reminds us that the power of wisdom forecloses the power of predicting the future. We can only gain insight and wisdom from events in the past. Much like the owl I saw at the protest, I would never have guessed that it would be able to fly away. But the event did not just happen; it was no deus ex machina. The owl got away due to the coordination, experience, spirit, and power of the protestors. The freedom was both an act of insurrection against the police, and the results of countless hours of organizing and communicating. Our current moment is similar. In the early months of the Trump administration, the future seems as unstable as at any time in my life. The institutions of government are in disarray and in conflict with each other; executive orders are being released that are both contradictory and confusing. The ground is shaking, or to put in more accurately, it is being shaken. And it is intentional.

As scholars, activists, and teachers interested in topics of social justice, urban politics, and radical politics, this means thinking about learning from the past; to look to theoretical understandings of the past to guide us in our actions and strategies as we move forward. But we must avoid being too beholden to the past that we do not theorize and try to understand the ways in which the present differs from it. Marx famously said "The philosophers have only interpreted the world, in various ways; the point is to change it." He was right. We need to marshal theory and philosophy and social sciences and turn them into tools to move us toward a more liberatory world. But we have to remember that right now the future is unwritten.

One of the lessons I hope that everyone takes from Food Not Bombs, Homes Not Jails, and the other anarchist homeless activists whose stories this book explores, is that we do not need massive numbers to push back, to resist, and to change things in this world. We must learn to accept and embrace being ungovernable. To refuse to accept that the past forecloses the future. Remember that the elites fear us. Now let's give them something to be really afraid of!

In lieu of a traditional conclusion, I want to end this book by putting together a series of "theses on homelessness, public space, and urban resistance". These short theses are a distillation of my thoughts and arguments regarding these topics after years of research, activism, and engagement in the field. I do not make this as an expert attempting to foreclose conversation, but instead as an opening of a dialogue. As we move forward in the era of Trump, we need to engage with many of the ideas that are at the core of the theses and this book. As activists, teachers, and researchers (and hopefully all three) we need to remember that thinking and acting are not mutually exclusive activities. Our actions must be guided by deep theorizing and thinking about power and change; and our thoughts must constantly be altered by the experiences of our actions.

Thesis 1: struggle over public space is central to revolutionary change

Donald Trump ran, in part, as a tough-on-crime, public-order candidate. His concern with addressing the "American carnage" in urban centers, as he called it, means that he is defining his presidency, at least in some part, through optics of order. Public space is always a central location for struggle and for political movements, but under regimes that are primarily focused on order they play an even larger role. The lessons from this book on Frank Jordan in San Francisco can be applied equally to Donald Trump. With Frank Jordan, Food Not Bombs and homeless activists were able to disrupt public space and undermine the mayor's ability to claim he had brought "order" to the public. In addition, because he was so concerned with public order, he often overreacted to protests, and the aggressive response from the police allowed activists to control the media narrative and frame the issue of homelessness in ways that were most beneficial to their goals. Similarly, Donald Trump has already shown the willingness to overreact and overreach—as we see with his Muslim visa ban—and that overreaching allows for protestors to take control of the narratives from him.

Thesis 2: the city plays a central role in modern capitalist economics

Part of Donald Trump's success as a candidate was on appealing to the economic and racial anxieties of suburban and rural white voters. In many of these areas—including the so-called rust belt—the economic shifts of capitalism since the 1980s have left entire swaths of the country behind. This result is similar to that of the Brexit vote in the UK, where it was largely rural and suburban areas that supported leaving the EU, whereas urban areas did not. Part of the split between these two regions is that urban spaces have seen massive economic gains, while rural areas have not. This is, I would argue, at least in part to the shift towards a service economy. Since urban areas have a high density of residents, the service economy has more space to grow and, when combined with a service economy oriented towards the wealthy and tourists, service work can provide a financial backbone to a city in the way that it cannot in rural areas. Another primary reason is that under neoliberalism and economic globalization, we have seen the construction of cosmopolitan cities—like New York, San Francisco, London, and Hong Kong—where global capital has been filtered. In this broader economic system the wealth of rural areas has increasingly been centralized within large cities, which also helps explain the massive inequality that exists within them.

The influx of wealth and economic power has led to cities playing a central role in the global capitalist economy. Urban spaces are not only a location in which wealth, especially intellectual property, is produced; they are also outlets for capitalist accumulation. The process of gentrification and urban redevelopment is part of a broader capitalist project to recirculate wealth via rebuilding and constructing space. As economic power in cities grows, they become central nodes in global capital. The ability to occupy, control, and disrupt these spaces therefore has a ripple effect that impacts the entire global economy.

Lastly, and connected to the last theses, urban space is the most visible and public space within the country. Making cities resistant entities to the current administration provides a powerful public declaration against the current order. Having cities, for instance, becoming sanctuary cities not only provides material protection to undocumented migrants but is a powerfully public statement of dissent to the current regime's anti-immigrant policies. The optics of disagreement undermines the president's desire for order and spatial unity.

Thesis 3: the homeless are a revolutionary class

Defining the revolutionary class was one of the dominant tensions that existed between Marxists and anarchists during the first international, an association of Marxists and anarchists that lasted from 1864 to 1876. Marxists, following the lead of Marx, saw the working class as the revolutionary class. They argued that only the working class functions as a direct anti-thesis to the bourgeoisie and, as such, they had the power to eradicate the concept of private property. The anarchists, led by Bakunin, on the other side, argued that the poor, the homeless, and peasants functioned as the most revolutionary class. This group, which Marx defined as the *lumpenproletariat*, to anarchists had absolutely nothing to lose, and therefore had more of a willingness to burn everything to the ground. To Marx, since they had nothing, they were more likely to be bought off, as a need for survival, by the elites who could use them as a tool to undermine working-class solidarity.

As economic forces have developed over the twenty-first century and, increasingly after the supposed great recession that started in 2008, the working class in the United States is defined more and more via their precariousness. This precariousness was, of course, always there, as non-white, female, and poor workers had experienced this reality for the entirety of capitalist economic history, but the expansion of it to most workers in the economy marks a drastic shift. With this shift, the lines blurring the *proletariat* and the *lumpenproletariat* have begun to break down. When most people in the United States do not have the savings to cover the cost of a month's living, everyone is living paycheck to paycheck, and therefore on the chasm of homelessness.

As the lines blur between the two groups, we see a difference of degree between the precarious worker and the homeless, instead of a difference of kind, as Marx argued. This blurring means an ability to link the struggles of the homeless with those of most workers in the United States. Increasingly the struggle—as we move from factory production to service economies—is not around the means of production in the classic sense of factory ownership, but in shared access to the massive accumulation of wealth and a redistribution of these resources locally, nationally, and globally. The expansion of the homeless, and other precarious workers, as revolutionary actors also requires a rethinking of the productionist logic of radical politics—acceptance of the refusal to work, and the providing of wages for housework.

Thesis 4: homelessness is a site of struggle that opens up space for more radical liberation

The activists and scholars from the Sojourner Truth Organization, a multiracial worker-centered revolutionary organization that was formed in the late 1960s, argued that by focusing on certain locations—most notably the most exploited and marginalized workers—that the economic gains would ripple up and open up new spaces for struggle. For instance, in the late 1960s, due to the racial order of capital, that meant organizing and working with black workers. If black workers—the lowest paid and more precarious—saw economic gains and increased political power, that would lift the bottom and, in effect, improve the power of everyone. As the structure of capitalism has changed in the intervening years, it is important to re-explore the structure of American capitalism, as the homeless have increasingly become a class within the United States. By fighting for the economic and political rights of the homeless, we lift the bottom, those facing the most extreme poverty and political marginalization, and in doing so lift others and potentially open up space for new struggles.

REFERENCES

"11 Facts About Hunger in the US | DoSomething.org | Volunteer for Social Change." (n.d.). [dosomething.org]. Retrieved February 7, 2017, from https://www.dosomething.org/facts/11-facts-about-hunger-us.

Agamben, G. (1998). *Sovereign power and bare life*. Stanford: Stanford University Press.

Agamben, G. (2005). *State of exception*. Chicago: University of Chicago Press.

Amnesty International. (1994). "Amnesty International and The Write a Letter Campaign." Retrieved February 7, 2017, from https://www.foodnotbombs.net/amnesty_letter.html.

anonymous. (1988). "*Sept. 6, 1988 re: Food Not Bombs Arrests.*" Agnos archives San Francisco Public Library.

Arendt, H. (1998). *The human condition* (2nd ed). Chicago: University of Chicago Press.

Arnold, K. R. (2004). *Homelessness, citizenship, and identity: the uncanniness of late modernity*. Albany: State University of New York Press.

Barclay, E. (2014, February 27). "U.S. Lets 141 Trillion Calories of Food Go to Waste Each Year." *The Salt : NPR*. Retrieved February 7, 2017, from www.npr.org/sections/thesalt/2014/02/27/283071610/u-s-lets-141-trillion-calories-of-food-go-to-waste-each-year.

Bertolucci, B. (2003). *The Dreamers*. Recorded Picture Company, France.

Bey, H. (2003). *T.A.Z.: the temporary autonomous zone, ontological anarchy, poetic terrorism* (2nd rev. ed). New York: Autonomedia.

Black, B. (1986). *The abolition of work and other essays*. Port Townsend: Loompanics Unlimited.

Bodovitz, K. (1989, July 12). "Crowd Angry at City Move to Clear Plaza." *San Francisco Chronicle*, p. A1.

Bodovitz, K. & Miyasato, M. (1989, July 22). "Ban on Food Giveaway Upheld." *San Francisco Chronicle*, p. A3.

Brazil, E. (1930). "A Rock of Stability for Homeless." *San Francisco Chronicle*, p. B1.

Brenner, N. (2004). *New state spaces: urban governance and the rescaling of statehood*. Oxford: Oxford University Press.

Butler, C. T. L. & McHenry, K. (2000). *Food ot Bombs*. Tucson: See Sharp Press.

Caffentzis, G. (2013). *In letters of blood and fire: work, machines, and the crisis of capitalism.* Oakland: PM Press.

Catholic Worker Movement. (n.d.). "Aims and Means." Retrieved February 23, 2017, from www.catholicworker.org/cw-aims-and-means.html.

Chronicle Reporter (1993). "4 Arrested for Serving Food at S. F Protest of Homeless Plan." *San Francisco Chronicle,* p. A3.

Corr, A. (1999). *No trespassing! Squatting, rent strikes, and land struggles worldwide.* Cambridge, MA: South End Press.

Cothran, G. 1995. "Matrix's Happy Face." *San Francisco Weekly.* Retrieved July 3, 2010, from www.sfweekly.com/1995-03-22/news/matrix-s-happy-face/.

Crass, C. (1995). "Towards a non-violent society: a position paper on anarchism, social change and Food Not Bombs," *The Anarchist Library.* Retrieved February 7, 2017, from https://theanarchistlibrary.org/library/chris-crass-towards-a-non-violent-society-a-position-paper-on-anarchism-social-change-and-food.

Day, C. (2003). "Dual Power in the Selva Lacandon." In R. San Filippo (Ed.), *A new world in our hearts: eight years of writings from the Love and Rage Revolutionary Anarchist Federation.* Oakland: AK Press, pp. 17–31.

Day, D. (1981). *The long loneliness: the autobiography of Dorothy Day.* San Francisco: Harper & Row.

Day, R. J. F. (2005). *Gramsci is dead: anarchist currents in the newest social movements.* Ann Arbor: Pluto Press.

Del Casino, V. J. & Jocoy, C. L. (2008). "Neoliberal Subjectivities, the 'New' Homelessness, and Struggles over Spaces of/in the City." *Antipode,* 40(2), 192–199.

DeLeon, R. E. (1992). *Left coast city: progressive politics in San Francisco, 1975–1991.* Lawrence: University Press of Kansas.

Delgado, R., Winokur, Scott, & Allison, A. (1995, June 26). "Hundred Added To Patrols; Peace Reiging So Far—The United Nations at 50." *San Francisco Chronicle,* p. A1.

Dominick, B. (2002). "An Introduction to Dual Power Strategy." Retrieved February 7, 2017, from http://left-liberty.net/?p=265.

Edmondson, R. (2000). *Rising up: class war in America from the streets to the airwaves.* San Francisco: Librad Press.

Epstein, B. L. (1991). *Political protest and cultural revolution: nonviolent direct action in the 1970s and 1980s.* Berkeley: University of California Press.

Falconer, S. (2010, March). "Solidarity, Not Charity for New Orleans." *Utne Reader.* Retrieved February 7, 2017, from www.utne.com/politics/solidarity-not-charity-for-new-orleans.

Federici, S. (2012). *Revolution at point zero: housework, reproduction, and feminist struggle.* Oakland: PM Press.

Feldman, L. C. (2006). *Citizens without shelter: homelessness, democracy, and political exclusion.* Ithaca: Cornell University Press.

Fernandez, L. A. (2008). *Policing dissent: social control and the anti-globalization movement.* New Brunswick: Rutgers University Press.

Ferrell, J. (2001). *Tearing down the streets: adventures in urban anarchy* (1st ed). New York: Palgrave Macmillan.

Foucault, M. (1995). *Discipline and punish: the birth of the prison* (2nd Vintage Books ed). New York: Vintage Books.

Foucault, M. & Gordon, C. (1980). *Power/knowledge: selected interviews and other writings, 1972–1977* (1st American ed). New York: Pantheon Books.

Foucault, M., Harcourt, B. E., & Burchell, G. (2015). *The punitive society: lectures at the College de France 1972–1973*. New York: Palgrave Macmillan.

Gardner, A. & Lindstrom, P. (1997). "Police on the Homelessness Front Line: A Postmorten of San Francisco's Matrix Program." In M. L. Forst (Ed.), *The police and the homeless: creating a partnership between law enforcement and social service agencies in the development of effective policies and programs*. Springfield, IL.: Charles C. Thomas Press, pp. 98–117.

Glissant, É. & Wing, B. (1997). *Poetics of relation*. Ann Arbor: University of Michigan Press.

Gordon, B. (1988a). "Debate Grows Over Food Vs. Politics." San Francisco Chronicle, p. A3.

Gordon, B. (1988b, September 9). "Free Food Again in the Haight." *San Francisco Chronicle*, p. A5.

Gordon, U. (2008). *Anarchy alive! Anti-authoritarian politics from practice to theory*. Ann Arbor: Pluto Press.

Gowan, T. (2010). *Hobos, hustlers, and backsliders: homeless in San Francisco*. Minneapolis: University of Minnesota Press.

Graeber, D. (2009). *Direct action: an ethnography*. Oakland: AK Press.

Granahl, J. & Taylor, B. (1994). "Jordan's Matrix Numbers Called 'Hard to Believe'." *San Francisco Examiner*, p. A3.

Grant, K. (2013, June 24). "Americans hate their jobs and even perks don't help." Retrieved March 8, 2017, from www.today.com/money/americans-hate-their-jobs-even-perks-dont-help-6C10423977.

Hackworth, J. (2010). "Faith, Welfare, and the City: The Mobilization of Religious Organizations for Neoliberal Ends." *Urban Geography*, 31(6), 750–773.

Hackworth, J. R. (2007). *The neoliberal city: governance, ideology, and development in American urbanism*. Ithaca: Cornell University Press.

Halstuk, M. (1988, September 10). "Cease-Fire Declared in Free Food War." *San Francisco Chronicle*, p. A3.

Hardin, G. (1968). "The Tragedy of the Commons." *Science*, 162(3859), 1243–1248.

Hartman, C. W., Carnochan, S., & Hartman, C. W. (2002). *City for sale: the transformation of San Francisco* (Rev. and updated ed). Berkeley: University of California Press.

Harvey, D. (2011). *A brief history of neoliberalism (Reprinted)*. Oxford: Oxford University Press.

Harvey, D. (2013). *Rebel cities: from the right to the city to the urban revolution* (Paperback ed). London: Verso.

Hatfield, L. D., M. G. Glover, et al. (1995). "GG Park Sweep on Heels of Protest." *San Francisco Examiner*. A3.

Heynen, N. (2010). "Cooking up Non-violent Civil-disobedient Direct Action for the Hungry: 'Food Not Bombs' and the Resurgence of Radical Democracy in the US." *Urban Studies*, (476), 1225–1240.

Hobsbawm, E. J. (1996). *The age of revolution 1789–1848* (1st Vintage Books ed). New York: Vintage Books.

INCITE! (Ed.). (2007). *The revolution will not be funded: beyond the non-profit industrial complex*. Cambridge, Mass: South End Press.

James, S. (2012). *Sex, race and class: the perspective of winning: a selection of writings, 1952–2011*. Oakland: PM Press.

Johnson, C. (1989, July 14). "2 Civic Center Arrests—Crackdown on Free Soup." *San Francisco Chronicle*, p. A2.

Johnson, C. (1995). "Tougher Moves Against the Homeless: An Attempt to Clean up City for VIPs. *San Francisco Chronicle*, p. A4.

Katsiaficas, G. (1997). *The subversion of politics: European autonomous social movements and the decolonization of everyday life*. Atlantic Highlands, NJ: Humanities Press.

Katz, M. B. (1996). *In the shadow of the poorhouse: a social history of welfare in America* (10th anniversary ed, and updated). New York: Basic Books.

King, J. and Bowman, C. (1994). Matrix Program Pushes into Neighborhoods. *San Francisco Chronicle*, p. A1.

Kohn, M. (2003). *Radical space: building the house of the people*. Ithaca: Cornell University Press.

Kohn, M. (2013). "Privatization and Protest: Occupy Wall Street, Occupy Toronto, and the Occupation of Public Space in a Democracy." *Perspectives on Politics*, 11(1), 99–110.

Kropotkin, P. (1975). *Essential Kropotkin*. New York: W. W. Norton

Kropotkin, P. (2011). *Mutual aid: a factor of evolution*. Place of publication not identified: Freedom Pr.

Landauer, G. & Kuhn, G. (2010). *Revolution and other writings: a political reader*. Oakland: PM Press.

Lefebvre, H., Kofman, E., & Lebas, E. (1996). *Writings on cities*. Cambridge, Mass: Blackwell Publishers.

Lefebvre, H. & Nicholson-Smith, D. (2011). *The production of space* (Nachdr.). Cambridge, Mass: Blackwell Publishers.

Lehrman, S. (1995). "Homeless Roost at Mayor's Door: As Police Watch, Protesters Decry Park Sweeps." *San Francisco Examiner*, p. A3.

Levy, D. (1993). "Jordan Aide, 6 Cops Seize Food Activist". *San Francisco Chronicle*, p. A3.

Levy, D. (1994). "Matrix Housing Falls Short." San Francisco Chronicle, p. A19.

Levy, D. (1995). "Campers Get 3 Days to Vacate Golden Gate Park: Mayor Reveals Homeless Sweep Plan. *San Francisco Chronicle*, p. A15.

Lindsey, J. R. (2013). *The concealment of the state*. New York: Bloomsbury.

Linebaugh, P. (2009). *The Magna Carta manifesto: liberties and commons for all*. Berkeley: University of California Press.

Linebaugh, P. & Rediker, M. (2013). *The many-headed hydra: sailors, slaves, commoners, and the hidden history of the revolutionary Atlantic* (2nd ed). Boston: Beacon Press.

Lucas, G. (1999). *Star Wars Episode 1: The Phantom Menace* [Film]. Lucas Films.

Lynch, A. (1993, September 30). "Food Not Bombs Demonstration in S. F. Again Ends With Arrests: City Continues Crackdown Against Group that Distributes Free Meals to Homeless." *San Francisco Chronicle*, p. A30.

Markell, G. 1991. "City Hall Melee After Arrest of Food Distributor." *San Francisco Chronicle*, p. A3.

Marx, K. (1852). 18th Brunaire of Louis Bonaparte. Retrieved March 7, 2017, from https://www.marxists.org/archive/marx/works/download/pdf/18th-Brumaire.pdf.

McGarry, D. (2008). *"The Politics of Homelessness in San Francisco, 1988–12002."* Dissertation History. Palo Alto, California, Stanford University.

McHenry, K. (2012). *Hungry for peace: how you can help end poverty and war with Food Not Bombs*. Tucson: See Sharp Press.

McKanan, D. (2008). *The Catholic worker after Dorothy: practicing the works of mercy in a new generation*. Collegeville, Minn: Liturgical Press.

McPhail, C., Schweingruber, D., & McCarthy, J. D. (1998). "Policing Protest in the United States: 1960–1995." In D. della Porta & H. Reiter (Eds.). *Policing protest: the control of mass demonstrations in Western democracies*. Minneapolis, MN: University of Minnesota Press, pp. 49–69.

Mignolo, W. (2011). *The darker side of Western modernity: global futures, decolonial options*. Durham: Duke University Press.

Mitchell, D. (1995). "The End of Public Space? People's Park, Definitions of the Public, and Democracy." *Annals of the Association of American Geographers*, 85(1), 108–133.

Mitchell, D. (2003). *The right to the city: social justice and the fight for public space*. New York: Guilford Press.

Mitchell, D. & Heynen, N. (2009). "The Geography of Survival and the Right to the City: Speculations on Surveillance, Legal Innovation, and the Criminalization of Intervention." *Urban Geography*, 30(6), 611–632.

Murphy, S. (2009). "'Compassionate' Strategies of Managing Homelessness: Post-Revanchist Geographies in San Francisco." *Antipode*, 41(2), 305–325.

National Coalition for the Homeless. (n.d.). "Homelessness in America." Retrieved March 7, 2017, from http://nationalhomeless.org/about-homelessness/.

National Coalition for the Homeless. (2006). "Mental Illness and Homelessness." Retrieved March 7, 2017, from www.nationalhomeless.org/publications/facts/Mental_Illness.pdf.

National Coalition for the Homeless. (2007). "Addiction Disorders and Homelessness." Retrieved March 7, 2017, from www.nationalhomeless.org/publications/facts/addiction.pdf.

Nibert, D. A. (2002). *Animal rights/human rights: entanglements of oppression and liberation*. Lanham: Rowman & Littlefield.

Olson, J. (2004). *The abolition of white democracy*. Minneapolis: University of Minnesota Press.

Ostrom, E. (1990). *Governing the commons: the evolution of institutions for collective action*. Cambridge: Cambridge University Press.

Peñalver, E. M. and S. K. Katyal (2010). *Property outlaws: how squatters, pirates, and protesters improve the law of ownership*. New Haven, CT: Yale University Press.

Pickerill, J., & Chatterton, P. (2006). "Notes Towards Autonomous Geographies: Creation, Resistance and Self-Management as Survival Tactics." *Progress in Human Geography*, 30(6), 730–746.

Piven, F. F. (2006). *Challenging authority: how ordinary people change America*. Lanham, Md: Rowman & Littlefield Publishers.

Piven, F. F. & Cloward, R. A. (1979). *Poor people's movements: why they succeed, how they fail*. New York: Vintage books.

Piven, F. F. & Cloward, R. A. (1993). *Regulating the poor: the functions of public welfare* (Updated ed). New York: Vintage Books.

Poppendieck, J. (1999). *Sweet charity? Emergency food and the end of entitlement.* New York: Penguin.

Pruijt, H. (2003). "Is the Institutionalization of Urban Movements Inevitable? A Comparison of the Opportunities for Sustained Squatting in New York City and Amsterdam." *International Journal of Urban Regional Research* 27(1): 133–157.

Rancière, J., & Corcoran, S. (2009). *Hatred of democracy* (Paperback ed). London: Verso.

Rancière, J. & Corcoran, S. (2010). *Dissensus: on politics and aesthetics.* London: Continuum.

Right to the City Alliance. (n.d.). "Mission & History." Retrieved March 8, 2017, from http://righttothecity.org/about/mission-history/.

Rojas, A. and Pimentel, B. (1995). "Crackdown in S. F. Park Delayed: No orders Yet to Evict Homeless. *San Francisco Chronicle*, p. A1.

Roy, A. (2003). "Paradigm of Propertied Citizenship: Transnational Techniques of Analysis." *Urban Affairs Review* 38(4): 463–491.

Russell, T. (2011). *A renegade history of the United States.* New York: Free Press.

Saunders, D. (1993a). "Civility Not Crime." *San Francisco Chronicle*, p. B8.

Saunders, D. (1993b). "Matrix A La Cart." *San Francisco Chronicle*, p. A24.

Shepard, B. H. & Smithsimon, G. (2011). *The beach beneath the streets: contesting New York City's public spaces.* Albany: State University of New York Press.

Smith, A. (2007). "Introduction: The Revolution Will Not be Funded." In INCITE! (Ed.), *The revolution will not be funded: beyond the non-profit industrial complex.* Boston, MA: South End Press, pp. 1–18.

Smith, N. (1996). *The New urban frontier: gentrification and the revanchist city.* Routledge: New York.

Sniegocki, J. (2005). "Creating a New Society: The Catholic Worker and the Community of the Ark." *Contemporary Justice Review*, 8(3), 295–306.

Soss, J., Fording, R. C., & Schram, S. (Eds.). (2011). *Disciplining the poor: neoliberal paternalism and the persistent power of race.* Chicago: University of Chicago Press.

Sparks, T. (2010). "Broke Not Broken: Rights, Privacy, and Homelessness in Seattle." *Urban Geography*, 31(6), 842–862.

Sparks, T. (2012). "Governing the Homeless in an Age of Compassion: Homelessness, Citizenship, and the 10–Year Plan to End Homelessness in King County Washington." *Antipode*, 44(4), 1510–1531.

Springer, S. (2011). "Public Space as Emancipation: Meditations on Anarchism, Radical Democracy, Neoliberalism and Violence." *Antipode*, 43(2), 525–562.

Staff, E. W. (1995). "Mad for Matrix: S. F.'s Program of Tough Love for the Homeless Sweeps into the Park, but it Still doesn't Fulfill the Mayor's Promise of a Bed for Everyone." *San Francisco Examiner.* A3.

Steinberg, M. (1994, November). "Homes Not Jails—House Building Group in San Francisco". *The Progressive.*

Thoburn, N. (2002). "Difference in Marx: the lumpenproletariat and the proletarian unnamable." *Economy and Society*, 31(3), 434–460.

Thompson, E. P. (1966). *The making of the English working class* (1st Vintage ed). New York: Vintage Books.

Tucker, R. C. (Ed.). (1978). *The Marx-Engels reader* (2nd ed). New York: Norton.

Vitale, A. (2009). *City of disorder how the quality of life campaign transformed New York politics.* New York: New York University Press.

Ward, C. (1973). *Anarchy in action.* New York: Harper & Row.

Ward, C. (1976). *Housing: an anarchist approach.* London: Freedom Press.

Wark, M. (2013). *The spectacle of disintegration* (1st ed). New York: Verso.

Wark, M. (2015). *The beach beneath the street: the everyday life and glorious times of the Situationist International.* New York: Verso.

Warshawsky, D. N. (2010). "New Power Relations Served Here: The Growth of Food Banking in Chicago." *Geoforum,* 41(5), 763–775.

Whitting, S. (1989, February 28). "Making Grub Not War." *San Francisco Chornicle,* pp. B3–4.

Willse, C. (2015). *The value of homelessness: managing surplus life in the United States.* Minneapolis: University of Minnesota Press.

Wilson, Y. (1999). "Squatters Try to Make Claim for Abandoned S. F. House." *San Francisco Chronicle.* Retrieved June 8, 2018 from www.sfgate.com/realestate/article/Squatters-Try-to-Make-Claim-for-Abandoned-S-F-2953396.php.

World Social Forum. (2005). "World Charter for the Right to the City." Unesco. Retrieved from http://portal.unesco.org/shs/en/files/8218/112653091412005_-_World_Charter_Right_to_City_May_051.doc/2005+-+World+Charter+Right+to+City+May+051.doc.

Wright, T. (1997). *Out of place: homeless mobilization, subcities, and contested landscapes.* Albany: State University of New York Press.

Zinn, H. (2000). "Why Food Not Bombs Book." Retrieved February 7, 2017, from https://www.foodnotbombs.net/howard_zinn_forward.html.

Zukin, S. (1987). "Gentrification: Culture and Capital in the Urban Core." *Annual Review of Sociology,* 13(1), 129–147.

INDEX

EU authorised representative for GPSR:
Easy Access System Europe, Mustamäe tee 50,
10621 Tallinn, Estonia
gpsr.requests@easproject.com

www.ingramcontent.com/pod-product-compliance
Lightning Source LLC
Chambersburg PA
CBHW052011270326
41929CB00015B/2870